BON APPÉTIT®
Light, Fresh & Easy

Bon Appétit®
Light, Fresh & Easy

THE CONDÉ NAST PUBLICATIONS INC.

Light, Fresh & Easy

Introduction

When the time came to name this collection of outstanding recipes from *Bon Appétit,* we thought of its title in a flash. After all, the words "light," "fresh" and "easy" are three of the adjectives we encounter most often when our readers write to let us know what kinds of dishes they want.

"I'm trying to serve lighter meals to everyone in my family these days," one letter might say. Another correspondent might add something along the lines of, "How about more ideas for all the fresh produce I find in my local farmers' market?" And time and again we'll receive this straightforward plea from subscribers: "Please make it easy!"

Of course, in issue after issue of *Bon Appétit,* we aim to deliver on all such requests.

The many light recipes we feature reflect today's widespread interest in healthful eating. In recent years, we've all learned the importance of reducing our intake of calories, fat, cholesterol, sugar and sodium, while increasing the amounts we eat of such beneficial foods as complex carbohydrates, cruciferous vegetables (the cabbage and broccoli family) and certain types of seafood. What we at the magazine find most interesting is that such healthful eating habits, once categorized under that dismal word "diet," have now become part of the everyday cooking habits of even the most sophisticated chefs.

Fresh, of course, goes hand in hand with light. Ingredients harvested at their peak and cooked in simple ways that highlight their inherent goodness can't help but be better for you.

Yet, try though all of us might to achieve those fresh and light ideals in our daily cooking, sometimes our busy schedules conspire against us. That is why our readers need easy recipes, and why we include so many of them on our pages every month. And even our quickest, simplest recipes are models of excellence that you could proudly serve to your most honored guests.

Which is why we have no hesitation in welcoming you to this collection of light, fresh and easy recipes with a salutation that has long been synonymous with good eating: *Bon Appétit!*

BON APPÉTIT®

Light, Fresh & Easy

CONTENTS

Appetizers & Beverages

Perk up your senses with the lively colors and aromas—and the fresh tastes and textures—of dishes designed to create a feeling of happy anticipation. In this chapter, you'll find a wide array of easy recipes including Melon with Port and Mint, Sun-dried Tomato Aioli Dip with Crudités, and New Potatoes Stuffed with Smoked Salmon and Horseradish. Add a Raspberry Freeze or a mug of Hot Spiced Wine, and even the most casual meal begins in gala fashion.

Appetizers

SUN-DRIED TOMATO AIOLI DIP WITH CRUDITÉS

20 SERVINGS

6 garlic cloves, peeled, halved
½ teaspoon salt
12 oil-packed sun-dried tomatoes, drained, patted dry, chopped
2 cups nonfat cottage cheese
⅓ cup plain nonfat yogurt
½ cup low-fat mayonnaise
  Salt

Assorted fresh vegetables

Place garlic on cutting board. Sprinkle with ½ teaspoon salt. Using flat side of knife, crush garlic. Add sun-dried tomatoes; mince to coarse paste. Puree cottage cheese in processor. Add yogurt and mayonnaise and blend well. Add garlic paste; process to blend. Season with salt. (*Can be made 1 day ahead. Chill.*)
Serve aioli with vegetables.

GRILLED EGGPLANT, RED BELL PEPPER AND ARUGULA ROLLS

6 SERVINGS

¼ cup balsamic vinegar
¼ cup olive oil
  Salt and pepper
2 small eggplants (1 pound each), cut lengthwise into ¼-inch-thick slices

4 red bell peppers

2 bunches arugula
½ cup (about) pine nuts, toasted

Prepare barbecue (medium heat). Whisk together vinegar and oil. Season with salt and pepper. Brush both sides of eggplant slices with ¼ cup vinaigrette. Grill until cooked through, turning occasionally, about 4 minutes per side. Remove from grill; brush with ¼ cup vinaigrette. Cool.
Grill bell peppers until blackened on all sides. Wrap in paper bag and let stand 10 minutes. Peel and seed peppers. Cut into ¼-inch strips. Season with salt and pepper. (*Can be made 1 day ahead. Cover; chill eggplant and bell peppers separately.*)
Place eggplant slices on work surface. Place 4 bell pepper strips on 1 end of each eggplant slice; top with 2 to 4 arugula sprigs, allowing peppers and arugula to extend beyond both sides of eggplant. Sprinkle pine nuts atop arugula. Roll eggplant up. Place seam side down on platter. (*Can be prepared 4 hours ahead. Cover.*)

SPICY MUSSELS IN WHITE WINE

Serve garlic toast with this to mop up all the savory broth.

6 APPETIZER SERVINGS

⅓ cup olive oil
½ onion, thinly sliced
4 large garlic cloves, chopped
2 teaspoons fennel seeds
1 teaspoon dried crushed red pepper

½ teaspoon salt
1 cup dry white wine
2 ¼-inch-thick lemon slices
½ cup chopped fresh parsley
2½ pounds fresh mussels, scrubbed,
    debearded
    Pepper
½ cup chopped seeded tomatoes

Heat oil in heavy large pot over medium-high heat. Add onion, garlic, fennel seeds, crushed red pepper and salt; sauté until onion is light brown, about 4 minutes. Add wine, lemon slices and ¼ cup parsley; bring to boil. Add mussels. Cover pot and cook until mussel shells open, stirring once to rearrange mussels, about 6 minutes; discard any mussels that do not open. Using slotted spoon, transfer mussels to large shallow bowl. Boil broth in pot until reduced to 1 cup, about 3 minutes; season to taste with pepper. Pour broth over mussels. Sprinkle tomatoes and remaining parsley over.

GARLIC UPDATE

The medical community has a few good reasons why you should increase your intake of garlic. Folk medicine has long ascribed curative powers to the "stinking rose," and recent studies show that certain sulfur compounds found in garlic can play a role in reducing blood pressure, lowering cholesterol and triglyceride levels, enhancing the immune system's response to disease and inhibiting the formation of carcinogens and the spread of cancers.

Encouraged by such reports, consumers are buying deodorized garlic dietary supplements like never before—and paying premium prices for them. But one of the best and most sensibly priced ways to enjoy garlic's benefits remains cooking with the fresh stuff on a regular basis. The same health-improving compounds also exist in the aromatic bulb's close cousins: shallots, onions, scallions and chives.

MEXICAN OYSTERS

MAKES 12

3 plum tomatoes, seeded, diced
3 green onions, chopped
⅓ cup chopped fresh cilantro
2 tablespoons olive oil
2 teaspoons ground cumin
1 jalapeño chili, seeded, chopped
    Salt and pepper

12 fresh oysters, shucked,
    left on half shell
    Crusty French bread

Combine first 6 ingredients in medium bowl. Season to taste with salt and pepper. Let stand 30 minutes.

Preheat broiler. Arrange oysters on broilerproof pan. Spoon salsa over oysters, dividing evenly. Broil until heated through, about 5 minutes. Serve with bread to soak up juices.

PORTOBELLO MUSHROOMS AND ROASTED PEPPERS WITH SOY-BALSAMIC VINAIGRETTE

Arrange the portobello mushrooms and roasted peppers atop greens as part of an antipasto platter, rounding out the selection with assorted cheeses, prosciutto, salami and olives.

6 SERVINGS

1 red bell pepper
1 green bell pepper
1 yellow bell pepper

3 tablespoons olive oil
2 6- to 7-inch-diameter portobello mushrooms, stemmed, caps cut into ¼-inch-wide slices
3 garlic cloves, minced
1½ teaspoons minced fresh rosemary
1½ teaspoons minced fresh sage

8 cups mixed baby greens
Soy-Balsamic Vinaigrette (see recipe)

Char peppers over gas flame or in broiler until blackened on all sides. Wrap in paper bag and let stand 10 minutes. Peel and seed peppers. Cut peppers into ¼-inch-wide strips. *(Peppers can be prepared 1 day ahead. Cover and refrigerate.)*

Heat oil in large nonstick skillet over medium-high heat. Add mushrooms and garlic and sauté until tender, about 4 minutes. Add rosemary and sage and stir until fragrant, about 30 seconds. Remove from heat. Cool to room temperature.

Arrange greens on large platter. Top with mushrooms and peppers. Drizzle lightly with vinaigrette.

SOY-BALSAMIC VINAIGRETTE

MAKES ABOUT ½ CUP

3 tablespoons balsamic vinegar
1 tablespoon soy sauce
¼ teaspoon dried crushed red pepper
⅓ cup olive oil
Salt and pepper

Whisk first 3 ingredients in medium bowl to blend. Gradually whisk in oil. Season with salt and pepper. *(Can be made 1 day ahead. Cover; chill. Bring to room temperature and rewhisk before using.)*

CALLING ALL SNACKERS

Potato chips are king of the snacking world. But when the average American consumes more than six pounds of chips a year, the nation's health takes a deep-fried pounding. Frito-Lay can help reduce some of that fat with their new Baked Potato Crisps. With a unique, nutty taste, these chips will satisfy all noshers and add only 1.5 grams of fat and 110 calories per serving—a realistic 12 chips (although 20 would be better).

Melon with Port and Mint

This innovative and refreshing dish is just right for warm-weather parties. Use only one variety of melon or an assortment, but be sure they are the ripest available.

10 SERVINGS

⅓ cup water
4 tablespoons minced fresh mint
3 tablespoons sugar

⅓ cup tawny or ruby port
2 to 3 melons (such as honeydew, cantaloupe, crenshaw or casaba), peeled, seeded, sliced
Fresh mint sprigs

Combine ⅓ cup water, 2 tablespoons minced mint and sugar in small saucepan. Stir over low heat until sugar dissolves. Bring to simmer. Remove from heat. Cover; let syrup stand at room temperature at least 2 hours or overnight.

Strain syrup into small bowl. Stir in port and 2 tablespoons minced fresh mint. Arrange melon slices on platter. Pour port syrup over. Cover and chill 2 hours. Garnish with mint sprigs.

Caviar Pie

16 SERVINGS

Nonstick vegetable oil spray
1 small onion, finely chopped
½ teaspoon sugar
10 hard-boiled eggs, peeled
¼ cup low-fat mayonnaise
2 tablespoons sweet pickle relish
1 8-ounce "brick" Neufchâtel cheese (reduced-fat cream cheese), room temperature
1 tablespoon milk

8 ounces caviar (preferably 2 or more colors)
Lemon slices
Chopped parsley
Assorted crackers

Spray 9-inch-diameter tart pan with removable bottom or 9-inch-diameter springform pan with vegetable oil spray. Combine onion and sugar in medium bowl. Place 10 whites and 6 yolks in processor (reserve remaining yolks for another use). Chop coarsely. Add mayonnaise and relish and process just until combined (do not overmix to paste). Add to bowl with onion and blend well. Spread over bottom of prepared pan. Refrigerate 15 minutes.

Combine Neufchâtel cheese and milk in processor. Blend well. Drop cheese mixture by teaspoonfuls over chilled egg layer and spread gently to cover. Refrigerate until firm, about 1 hour. (*Can be prepared 1 day ahead. Cover and keep refrigerated.*)

Spoon caviar decoratively atop cheese layer. Garnish with lemon slices and parsley. Press bottom of tart pan up or remove sides of springform pan, releasing pie. Place pie on platter; surround with crackers.

THE BEGINNING AND THE END

Kevin Morrissey and Barry Bluestein are former owners of a cookbook store, so they know what makes a good, user-friendly cookbook. They also know how to cook light. In *The 99% Fat-Free Book of Appetizers and Desserts* (Doubleday, 1996, $27.50), they supply readers with a creative array of recipes for low-fat starters and finales. To do this, Morrissey and Bluestein broke down traditional recipes and rebuilt them without unnecessary fats from meats, poultry, seafood, dairy products and chocolate until each serving was left with no more than one gram of fat. But they kept all the taste in dishes like spicy chicken salad with peppercorns, garlic and water chestnuts; spinach quenelles in tomato sauce; and banana bread cake. The section on stocking a nearly fat-free pantry makes creating healthful meals even easier.

NEW POTATOES STUFFED WITH SMOKED SALMON AND HORSERADISH

MAKES 24

12 baby red-skinned potatoes
1 tablespoon olive oil

3½ ounces smoked salmon, finely chopped
2 tablespoons sour cream
2 teaspoons minced red onion
1 teaspoon drained capers
½ teaspoon prepared white horseradish
Pepper

½ ounce thinly sliced smoked salmon, cut into 24 squares
Additional drained capers

Preheat oven to 400°F. Cut potatoes in half crosswise. Mix with oil in bowl. Place cut side down on heavy large baking sheet. Bake potatoes until just tender, about 25 minutes. Cool completely.

Mix 3½ ounces salmon, sour cream, onion, 1 teaspoon capers and horseradish in small bowl. Season with pepper. (*Potatoes and salmon mixture can be made 1 day ahead. Cover separately and chill.*)

Cut thin slice off rounded end of each potato so that potatoes will stand upright. Turn potatoes over. Using melon baller or small spoon, scoop out some of center of each potato. Spoon 1 teaspoon filling into each. Garnish each with smoked salmon and caper. (*Can be prepared 2 hours ahead. Cover and chill.*)

Beverages

FRESH MINT AND GINGER LEMONADE

This distinctive fat-free drink is a great change of pace from coffee or tea.

4 SERVINGS

½ cup (packed) chopped fresh
    mint leaves
⅓ cup chopped fresh ginger
⅓ cup honey
2 cups boiling water
⅓ cup fresh lemon juice
1½ cups (about) cold water

   Ice cubes
   Fresh mint leaves
   Lemon slices

Combine chopped mint, ginger and honey in medium bowl. Add boiling water. Let steep 30 minutes. Strain into 4-cup glass measuring cup, pressing on solids to extract liquid. Add lemon juice and enough cold water to measure 4 cups total. *(Can be prepared 1 day ahead. Cover and refrigerate.)*

Fill glasses with ice cubes. Add lemonade. Garnish with mint leaves and lemon slices and serve.

RASPBERRY FREEZE

4 SERVINGS

2 ½-pint baskets fresh raspberries
2 cups raspberry juice or other
   berry juice
3 tablespoons (or more) honey
8 to 10 ice cubes
4 orange slices

Puree raspberries, juice and 3 tablespoons honey in blender. Add more honey, if desired. Add ice cubes; puree until frothy. Pour into glasses. Garnish with orange slices; serve immediately.

CLEARING UP THE WATERS

The human body is more than two-thirds water and depends on fluids for its well-being. To help people make smart water choices, the San Pellegrino mineral water company has produced a free brochure called the *Guide to Bottled Water.* The pamphlet clarifies the different categories of flavored, sparkling, spring, mineral and seltzer waters and explains how the presence or absence of minerals, carbonation and trace elements affects overall quality and taste. To receive a copy, send a business-size S.A.S.E. to San Pellegrino USA, Radio City Station, Box 1367, Department PR, New York, NY 10101.

HOT SPICED WINE

Either red wine or a nonalcoholic Cabernet Sauvignon works well in this version of vin chaud, *a popular French drink. This recipe is just the thing to take the chill off a brisk fall day.*

6 SERVINGS

1 25.4-ounce bottle nonalcoholic Cabernet Sauvignon wine (such as Ariél) or one 750-ml bottle dry red wine
2 small oranges, cut into ¼-inch-thick slices
1 lemon, thinly sliced
½ cup fresh orange juice
6 tablespoons sugar
20 whole cloves

Combine wine, 5 orange slices, 3 lemon slices, fresh orange juice, sugar and 8 whole cloves in heavy medium saucepan. Bring to boil. Remove from heat, cover and let stand 30 minutes. Strain. Return to same saucepan. *(Can be made 1 day ahead. Cover; chill. Rewarm before filling Thermos or before serving.)*

Stud 6 orange slices with 2 cloves each. Divide orange slices and 6 lemon slices among cups. Pour spiced wine over.

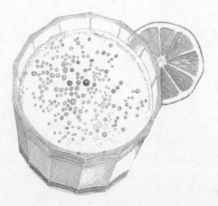

Soups & Salads

Some of the best soups and salads display a simplicity of taste and texture that results when the finest fresh ingredients are combined with a light, sure hand. You'll find this deft approach in such generous bowlfuls as Great Gazpacho, Tortilla Soup with Tomatoes and Smoked Turkey, and Chilled Carrot Soup with Garden Herbs, and in salads like Mixed Greens with Raspberry Vinaigrette or Smoked Turkey Salad with Bing Cherries and Hazelnuts. Whether served to start a meal or as main courses in their own right, such dishes–however light–satisfy completely.

Soups

Low-Fat Vegetable Soup

8 SERVINGS

3 medium zucchini, sliced
2 medium carrots, sliced
10 mushrooms, sliced
1 medium onion, sliced
1 10-ounce russet potato, peeled,
  cut into 1-inch pieces
3 14½-ounce cans vegetable broth
3 cups canned crushed tomatoes
  with added puree
1 14½-ounce can stewed tomatoes
3 tablespoons chopped fresh parsley
2 tablespoons chopped fresh
  cilantro
1 tablespoon chopped garlic
1 teaspoon dried basil
1 teaspoon dried oregano
  Salt and pepper

Additional chopped fresh parsley

Combine zucchini, carrots, mushrooms, onion and potato in heavy large Dutch oven. Add vegetable broth, crushed tomatoes, stewed tomatoes, 3 tablespoons parsley, cilantro, garlic, basil and oregano. Bring mixture to boil. Reduce heat, cover and simmer until vegetables are tender, about 30 minutes.

Strain cooking liquid into large saucepan; reserve vegetables. Place 3 cups vegetables in blender. Add ¼ cup cooking liquid. Puree until smooth. Stir puree into remaining cooking liquid in saucepan. Return remaining vegetables to cooking liquid. Season to taste with salt and pepper. (*Can be prepared 5 days ahead. Cover and refrigerate.*)

Bring soup to simmer. Ladle into bowls. Sprinkle with additional parsley.

Curly Endive and Bean Soup

You could use two peeled and diced potatoes instead of the beans.

6 TO 8 SERVINGS

3 tablespoons olive oil
6 large garlic cloves, chopped
⅔ cup diced ham (about 3 ounces)
2 large heads curly endive, cut into
  bite-size pieces
6 cups canned low-salt chicken
  broth
1 15- to 16-ounce can Great
  Northern beans, drained
  Salt and pepper

Heat oil in heavy large Dutch oven over medium heat. Add garlic; sauté until just tender, about 3 minutes. Add ham; stir 1 minute. Add endive, broth and beans; simmer until endive wilts and is tender but still bright green, about 10 minutes. Season with salt and pepper.

CHILLED CARROT SOUP WITH GARDEN HERBS

This lovely summer soup has a rich, smooth texture even though it contains no cream.

6 SERVINGS

6 tablespoons olive oil
5 large carrots, thinly sliced
2½ cups thinly sliced onions
1 teaspoon dried thyme
1 teaspoon golden brown sugar
½ teaspoon ground nutmeg
4 cups canned chicken broth
¼ cup orange juice
  Salt and pepper
  Chopped fresh chives

Heat olive oil in large saucepan over medium heat. Add carrots and onions and sauté 4 minutes. Add thyme, brown sugar and nutmeg; sauté until vegetables are tender, about 6 minutes. Add chicken broth. Cover pot; simmer until carrots are very soft, about 25 minutes. Using slotted spoon, transfer vegetables to processor. Add ¼ cup cooking liquid. Puree vegetables until smooth. Return puree to pot. Stir in orange juice. Season to taste with salt and pepper. Chill. *(Can be made 1 day ahead. Keep refrigerated.)* Sprinkle with chives.

TOMATO-FENNEL SOUP WITH GREMOLATA

Gremolata is a parsley and lemon peel mixture commonly used in Italy with osso buco.

4 SERVINGS

SOUP

2 tablespoons olive oil
2 cups finely chopped fennel bulb
1 28-ounce can Italian-style tomatoes, drained, juices reserved
2⅔ cups chicken stock or canned low-salt broth
¼ cup fresh lemon juice
  Salt and pepper

GREMOLATA

2 tablespoons chopped fresh parsley
2 tablespoons chopped fennel fronds
4 teaspoons minced garlic
1½ teaspoons grated lemon peel

FOR SOUP: Heat oil in heavy large Dutch oven over medium heat. Add chopped fennel bulb; sauté until tender but not brown, about 6 minutes. Add drained tomatoes; sauté 5 minutes. Add reserved tomato juices, stock and lemon juice. Cover; simmer 15 minutes. Puree soup in blender in batches until smooth. Return to pan. Season with salt and pepper. *(Can be made 1 day ahead. Cover and refrigerate.)*

FOR GREMOLATA: Mix all ingredients in small bowl.

Bring soup to simmer. Ladle into bowls. Stir spoonful of gremolata into each bowl and serve.

GREAT GAZPACHO

8 TO 10 SERVINGS

4 cups tomato juice
1 pint purchased fresh mild salsa
2 red bell peppers, seeded,
    chopped
1 cucumber, peeled, seeded,
    chopped
1 cup onion- and garlic-seasoned
    croutons
½ cup low-salt canned chicken broth
⅓ cup chopped fresh cilantro
4 large garlic cloves
2 tablespoons balsamic or red wine
    vinegar
1 tablespoon olive oil
1 teaspoon ground cumin
    Hot pepper sauce (such as
    Tabasco)
    Salt and pepper

Working in batches, blend all ingredients except hot sauce in processor to coarse puree. Transfer gazpacho to large bowl. Season to taste with hot sauce, salt and pepper. Refrigerate until well chilled, about 2 hours. (*Can be prepared 1 day ahead.*) Ladle into bowls and serve.

CHILLED YELLOW PEPPER AND WHITE BEAN SOUP

This superb starter has no cream and just one tablespoon of oil.

4 SERVINGS

3 yellow, orange or red bell peppers

1 tablespoon olive oil
1 small onion, chopped
⅛ teaspoon dried crushed red
    pepper
2 14½-ounce cans low-salt chicken
    broth
1 15- to 16-ounce can cannellini
    (white kidney beans), rinsed,
    drained
    Salt and pepper

1 bunch fresh arugula, sliced

Char bell peppers over gas flame or in broiler until blackened on all sides. Place in paper bag and let stand 10 minutes. Peel, seed and chop peppers.

Heat oil in heavy medium saucepan over medium-high heat. Add onion and sauté until tender, about 5 minutes. Add bell peppers and crushed red pepper and sauté 1 minute. Add broth and cannellini. Bring to boil. Reduce heat, cover and simmer 15 minutes. Strain vegetables, reserving broth. Transfer vegetables to processor; puree. Gradually mix in 2 cups reserved broth. Transfer puree to bowl. Stir in remaining broth. Season with salt and pepper. Cover; chill until cold. (*Can be made 1 day ahead. Keep chilled.*)

Ladle soup into bowls. Top with generous amount of arugula and serve.

Lemon Chicken Soup with Fresh Spinach and Farfalle

2 tablespoons olive oil
1 large onion, chopped
2 large garlic cloves, finely chopped
3 celery stalks, chopped
2 carrots, diced
1 large red bell pepper, chopped
8 cups (or more) canned low-salt
    chicken broth
2 cups dried farfalle (bow-tie) pasta

2 cups diced cooked chicken
2 tablespoons fresh lemon juice
2 teaspoons grated lemon peel
½ 10-ounce package ready-to-use
    spinach leaves (about 6 cups)
    Salt and pepper

Grated Parmesan cheese

Heat oil in heavy large pot over medium heat. Add onion and garlic and stir 1 minute. Add celery, carrots and red bell pepper and sauté until vegetables are tender, about 8 minutes. Add 8 cups broth and bring soup to boil. Reduce heat to medium-low; simmer to blend flavors, about 20 minutes. Add pasta and simmer until pasta is tender, stirring occasionally, about 10 minutes.

Mix chicken, lemon juice and lemon peel into soup. Add spinach. Simmer until spinach wilts but is still bright green, stirring occasionally, about 3 minutes. Thin soup with additional chicken broth, if desired. Season soup to taste with salt and pepper.

Ladle soup into bowls. Serve, passing cheese separately.

Roasted Butternut Squash Soup

Nonstick vegetable oil spray
1 2-pound butternut squash, halved
    lengthwise, seeded
2 cups (about) canned low-salt
    chicken broth
    Pinch of grated nutmeg
1 cup nonfat milk
    Salt and pepper
    Nonfat sour cream (optional)
    Chopped fresh chives or green
    onions (optional)

Preheat oven to 375°F. Spray 13x9x2-inch glass baking dish with vegetable oil spray. Place squash cut side down in prepared dish. Pierce each squash half several times with toothpick or skewer. Bake until squash is tender, about 45 minutes.

Using large spoon, scrape squash into processor; discard peel. Add 1½ cups broth and nutmeg and puree until smooth. Transfer puree to heavy large saucepan. Mix in milk and enough broth to thin to desired consistency. Stir soup over medium heat until heated through. Season to taste with salt and pepper. Ladle soup into bowls. Top with dollop of sour cream and chives, if desired.

CHILLED CUCUMBER-YOGURT SOUP WITH RADISHES

This pretty and refreshing soup—flavored with curry, cumin, ginger and garlic—is quick to prepare: Just put everything in the blender and puree it.

6 SERVINGS

2¼ cups plain yogurt
1¼ pounds pickling cucumbers, trimmed, peeled, cut into 1-inch pieces
2 garlic cloves, minced
1½ teaspoons salt
1½ teaspoons ground cumin
1½ teaspoons curry powder
¼ teaspoon (generous) ground ginger

Thinly sliced radishes

Combine yogurt, cucumbers, garlic, salt, cumin, curry and ginger in blender. Puree until smooth. Strain through fine sieve into large bowl. Refrigerate until well chilled, about 2 hours. (*Can be prepared 1 day ahead. Keep refrigerated.*)

Ladle soup into bowls. Top with radishes and serve.

TORTILLA SOUP WITH TOMATOES AND SMOKED TURKEY

6 SERVINGS

1½ tablespoons olive oil
1½ cups chopped onion
1 tablespoon plus 2 teaspoons minced garlic
1 28-ounce can Italian plum tomatoes, drained, chopped
2¼ teaspoons dried oregano
1½ teaspoons ground cumin
¼ teaspoon dried crushed red pepper

6 cups canned vegetable broth
1 cup thinly sliced carrots
½ cup cubed red bell pepper
½ cup cubed yellow bell pepper
½ cup cubed celery
1½ cups thinly sliced zucchini

¾ pound thinly sliced smoked turkey breast, cut into matchstick-size strips
Salt and pepper

Nonstick vegetable oil spray
7 corn tortillas (6-inch diameter), cut into ¼-inch-wide strips

½ cup packed fresh cilantro leaves
1 tablespoon grated lemon peel

1 cup grated Monterey Jack cheese
¾ cup shelled sunflower seeds
1 lemon, cut into 6 wedges

Heat oil in heavy large Dutch oven over medium-high heat. Add onion; sauté until tender, about 4 minutes. Add 1 tablespoon garlic; sauté 1 minute. Stir in tomatoes, oregano, cumin and dried red pepper. Simmer until thick, stirring often, about 10 minutes. Puree mixture in processor. Set aside.

Pour broth into Dutch oven; bring to simmer over medium heat. Add carrots, bell peppers and celery; cook until tender, about 6 minutes. Add zucchini;

cook 3 minutes. Add tomato mixture and turkey. Season with salt and pepper. (*Can be made 1 day ahead. Cover; chill.*)

Preheat oven to 350°F. Line large baking sheet with foil. Spray foil with vegetable oil spray. Arrange tortilla strips on prepared sheet. Bake until crisp and golden, turning once, about 18 minutes.

Combine cilantro, lemon peel and 2 teaspoons minced garlic in bowl. (*Tortilla strips and cilantro mixture can be made 4 hours ahead. Cover separately and let stand at room temperature.*)

Bring soup to simmer. Serve with tortilla strips, cilantro mixture, cheese, sunflower seeds and lemon as garnishes.

LAMB AND BARLEY SOUP

8 SERVINGS

1 tablespoon vegetable oil
2½ pounds meaty lamb neck bones
10 cups water
½ small cabbage, chopped
2 carrots, peeled, chopped
1 large onion, chopped
½ large rutabaga, peeled, chopped

⅔ cup pearl barley, rinsed
3 tablespoons instant beef bouillon granules
2 teaspoons dried thyme
2 bay leaves
Pinch of ground allspice
Salt and pepper

Heat oil in heavy large pot or Dutch oven over high heat. Add lamb bones; sauté until dark brown, about 10 minutes. Add remaining ingredients. Bring to boil. Reduce heat to medium; simmer until lamb, barley and all vegetables are tender and soup is thick, stirring occasionally, about 1 hour 30 minutes. Remove bay leaves. Season with salt and pepper.

FORTIFYING YOUR HEALTH

Tiny but crucial battles against free radicals—particles believed to lead to clogged arteries, weakened immune systems and cancer—are constantly being fought in the body. The best-known defense against these health-damaging particles is to load up on healthful food rich in antioxidants, the agents that may disarm free radicals naturally.

The Miracle Nutrient Cookbook (Simon & Schuster, 1995, $12), by Tamara Holt and Maureen Callahan, has one hundred recipes packed with vitamins C and E and other free-radical fighters such as beta-carotene and selenium. And the recipes—carrot and chickpea curry, bell pepper lasagna and broiled chicken with roasted-pepper sauce, to name a few—are so appealing that their disease-fighting power is just a bonus.

Appetizer & Side-Dish Salads

MIXED GREENS WITH RASPBERRY VINAIGRETTE

A simple way to serve all the best greens from the garden.

8 SERVINGS

3 tablespoons raspberry vinegar
1 tablespoon Dijon mustard
1 teaspoon minced garlic
½ teaspoon anchovy paste
⅓ cup olive oil
   Salt and pepper

8 cups mixed baby greens
   (about 7 ounces)
2 bunches arugula

Combine first 4 ingredients in medium bowl. Gradually whisk in olive oil. Season to taste with salt and pepper.

Combine mixed baby greens and arugula in large bowl. Toss with enough dressing to coat and serve.

CAROLINA COLESLAW

8 SERVINGS

½ cup distilled white vinegar
6 tablespoons sugar
6 tablespoons vegetable oil
2½ teaspoons dry mustard
1 teaspoon celery seeds
   Salt and pepper

1 medium cabbage (about 1¼ pounds), thinly sliced
1 large onion, thinly sliced
1 large green bell pepper, thinly sliced

Combine vinegar, sugar, oil, mustard and celery seeds in nonaluminum medium saucepan. Stir over medium heat until sugar dissolves and dressing comes to boil. Remove from heat. Season with salt and pepper. Cool completely.

Combine cabbage, onion and green pepper in large bowl. Add dressing; toss to coat. Cover; refrigerate until cold, tossing occasionally, at least 2 hours. (*Can be made 1 day ahead. Cover; keep refrigerated.*)

MIXED GREENS AND WALNUTS WITH BUTTERMILK DRESSING

6 SERVINGS

1 tablespoon fresh lime juice
1 tablespoon balsamic vinegar
½ teaspoon Dijon mustard
⅓ cup low-fat buttermilk
1 tablespoon walnut oil or olive oil
   Salt and pepper

8 ounces mixed baby greens
¼ cup walnut pieces, toasted
3 tablespoons chopped fresh parsley

Whisk lime juice, vinegar and mustard in medium bowl to blend. Gradually whisk in buttermilk, then oil. Season to taste with salt and pepper. (*Can be prepared 6 hours ahead. Cover and refrigerate.*)

Combine mixed greens, walnuts and parsley in large bowl. Toss with enough dressing to coat. Season to taste with salt and pepper and serve.

DON'T BE AFRAID OF THE DARK

Here's an easy-to-remember nutrition tip: Research shows that green vegetables with darker leaves have higher concentrations of fiber, iron, calcium and other nutrients and are richer in antioxidants (the essential nutrients believed to prevent cancer and heart disease) than their lighter cousins. For example, the *University of California at Berkeley Wellness Letter* points out that although iceberg lettuce is America's favorite leafy green vegetable, deeper-colored romaine lettuce is more nutritionally valuable, with six times the vitamin C and eight times the beta-carotene. Other dark vegetables to try in your next pasta dish or salad include kale, collard greens and dandelion greens.

GREEN BEAN, WATERCRESS AND RADISH SALAD

10 SERVINGS

2½ pounds green beans, trimmed

¼ cup fresh lemon juice
2 tablespoons distilled white vinegar
4 teaspoons Dijon mustard
½ cup olive oil
½ cup canned chicken broth
1 cup chopped watercress leaves
Salt and pepper

1 bunch watercress, ends trimmed
1½ cups thinly sliced radishes

Cook beans in large pot of boiling salted water until crisp-tender, about 5 minutes. Drain beans; rinse under cold water. Drain and pat dry.

Whisk lemon juice, vinegar and mustard in medium bowl to blend. Whisk in oil and broth. Add chopped watercress. Season with salt and pepper.

Toss beans, trimmed watercress and radishes in bowl with dressing.

TOMATO, ONION AND HEARTS OF PALM SALAD

4 TO 6 SERVINGS

¼ cup olive oil
3 tablespoons chopped fresh basil
  or 2 teaspoons dried
2 tablespoons white wine vinegar
1 pound plum tomatoes, cut into
  wedges
1 14-ounce can hearts of palm,
  drained, cut crosswise into
  1-inch pieces
1 medium onion, thinly sliced
  Salt and pepper

Whisk oil, basil and vinegar in medium bowl to blend. Add remaining ingredients and toss to blend. Season to taste with salt and pepper. Let salad stand at room temperature at least 30 minutes and up to 2 hours.

SWEET ORANGE, MINT AND OLIVE SALAD

This Moroccan-style salad is a flavorful part of any colorful buffet.

6 SERVINGS

½ teaspoon coriander seeds
½ teaspoon cumin seeds
⅓ cup brine-cured black olives
    (such as Kalamata), pitted
¼ cup fresh orange juice
¼ cup chopped fresh mint
3 green onions, chopped
¼ teaspoon sugar

5 medium navel oranges, peel and
    white pith removed
    Salt and pepper

Romaine lettuce leaves

Toast coriander seeds and cumin seeds in medium skillet over medium heat just until fragrant, about 2 minutes. Transfer spices to a heavy small plastic bag. Using flat side of knife, press on spices to crush coarsely. Transfer spices to large bowl. Add olives, orange juice, mint, green onions and sugar; stir to blend.

Cut oranges into ⅓-inch-thick rounds. Add orange rounds to olive mixture and stir gently to coat. Season to taste with salt and pepper. (*Can be prepared 1 hour ahead. Cover and refrigerate.*)

Arrange lettuce leaves on platter. Arrange orange mixture decoratively atop lettuce and serve.

WATERCRESS AND MUSHROOM SALAD WITH ASIAN DRESSING

Just a bit of intensely flavored Oriental sesame oil goes a long way in the dressing of this refreshing salad. To retain the crispness of the watercress, toss it with the remaining ingredients right before serving.

6 SERVINGS

2 tablespoons balsamic vinegar
1½ teaspoons grated orange peel
½ teaspoon Dijon mustard
¼ cup canned low-salt chicken broth
1 tablespoon Oriental sesame oil
1 tablespoon olive oil
    Salt and pepper

1¼ pounds large mushrooms, stems
    trimmed, caps thinly sliced
½ cup thinly sliced green onions

2 large bunches watercress, trimmed

Combine vinegar, orange peel and mustard in large bowl. Gradually whisk in broth, sesame oil and olive oil. Season dressing to taste with salt and pepper.

Place mushrooms and green onions in large bowl. Pour ¼ cup dressing over mushroom mixture. Toss to coat well. Let stand 45 minutes at room temperature. (*Can be made 4 hours ahead. Cover; chill.*)

Add watercress and remaining dressing to mushroom mixture and toss. Season salad to taste with salt and pepper. Serve salad immediately.

SESAME BROCCOLI SALAD

An easy side dish with a bit of Asian flavor.

6 SERVINGS

2 tablespoons soy sauce
2 tablespoons rice vinegar
2 tablespoons Oriental sesame oil
2 tablespoons honey
  Salt and pepper

12 cups broccoli florets (from 2 large
  bunches)

½ cup sesame seeds

Whisk soy sauce, vinegar, oil and honey in large bowl until blended. Season to taste with salt and pepper.

Steam broccoli florets until crisp-tender, about 5 minutes. Cool.

Stir sesame seeds in heavy large skillet over medium heat until golden, about 5 minutes. Transfer to small bowl; cool.

Mix broccoli and half of sesame seeds into dressing. Let marinate at room temperature at least 30 minutes or up to 2 hours, tossing occasionally.

Transfer broccoli to platter. Pour dressing over. Sprinkle with remaining sesame seeds.

NEW POTATO AND CUCUMBER SALAD WITH FRESH HERBS

8 SERVINGS

2¼ pounds red-skinned potatoes
2 medium cucumbers, peeled,
  seeded, diced
½ cup chopped red onion
1 cup plain low-fat yogurt
6 tablespoons chopped fresh dill
4 teaspoons chopped fresh mint
2 teaspoons minced garlic
  Salt and pepper

Cook potatoes in large pot of boiling salted water until tender, about 18 minutes. Drain potatoes; cool. Peel potatoes. Cut into ¾-inch cubes and place in large bowl. Add cucumbers and onion. Whisk all remaining ingredients in small bowl. Add to potatoes. Season with salt and pepper. (*Can be made 8 hours ahead; chill.*)

RICE SALAD WITH DILL AND BABY VEGETABLES

4 SERVINGS

4 ounces baby carrots (about 16),
  trimmed, halved lengthwise
8 ounces baby zucchini or baby
  pattypan squash, ends trimmed,
  halved
¾ cup long-grain white rice

½ cup plain low-fat yogurt
3 tablespoons chopped fresh dill
1½ tablespoons rice vinegar
1 teaspoon olive oil
  Salt and pepper
  Fresh dill sprigs (optional)

Blanch carrots in large pot of boiling salted water 1 minute. Add zucchini and cook 1 minute. Using slotted spoon, transfer vegetables to colander. Rinse under cold water; drain well. Add rice to same pot of boiling water. Cook until tender, about 15 minutes. Drain. Rinse under cold water; drain well. Cool to room temperature.

Mix rice, carrots and zucchini in

large bowl. Add yogurt, chopped dill, vinegar and oil. Toss to coat. Season to taste with salt and pepper. (*Can be prepared 6 hours ahead. Cover and refrigerate.*) Garnish with dill sprigs, if desired.

Main Course Salads

MEXICAN PASTA SALAD

For convenience, buy a roasted chicken from your market or favorite take-out place, remove the skin and toss the chicken meat with the cooked fusilli and vegetables.

8 SERVINGS

1¼ pounds fusilli pasta
1½ tablespoons plus ⅓ cup olive oil
1 2½-pound roasted chicken, skinned, meat shredded
4 large tomatoes, seeded, diced (about 4 cups)
3 cups corn kernels (fresh or frozen, thawed)
3 large carrots, thinly sliced on diagonal, slices cut lengthwise into thin strips
½ large red onion, chopped

2 tablespoons plus 1 teaspoon Dijon mustard
2 tablespoons plus 1 teaspoon fresh lime juice
2 jalapeño chilies, seeded, minced
1¼ teaspoons chili powder
1¼ teaspoons ground cumin
2 bunches fresh cilantro, coarsely chopped
Salt and pepper

Cook fusilli pasta in large pot of boiling salted water until just tender but still firm to bite. Drain. Rinse pasta with cold water to cool. Drain pasta well. Transfer pasta to large bowl. Add 1½ tablespoons olive oil and mix thoroughly to coat. Add shredded chicken, diced tomatoes, corn kernels, carrot strips and chopped onion and toss.

Mix Dijon mustard and fresh lime juice in small bowl. Gradually mix in remaining ⅓ cup olive oil. Mix in minced jalapeño chilies, chili powder and ground cumin. Add dressing and chopped fresh cilantro to salad and mix to blend. Season to taste with salt and pepper. (*Salad can be prepared 4 hours ahead. Cover and refrigerate.*)

POTATO AND SEAFOOD SALAD WITH TARRAGON

10 SERVINGS

3 pounds white-skinned potatoes
3 tablespoons white wine vinegar
Salt and pepper

1 tablespoon butter
10 ounces uncooked medium shrimp, peeled, halved lengthwise
10 ounces bay scallops
10 ounces crabmeat, drained, picked over

½ cup plus 2 tablespoons sour cream
5 tablespoons mayonnaise
5 green onions, minced
5 tablespoons minced fresh tarragon
Fresh tarragon sprigs

Place potatoes in heavy large saucepan. Add water to cover. Season generously with salt. Bring to boil. Cover and cook until potatoes are tender, about 25 minutes. Drain. Cool slightly. Peel potatoes. Cut potatoes in half lengthwise, then cut crosswise into ½-inch-thick pieces. Place half of potatoes in large bowl. Drizzle with 1 tablespoon vinegar. Season with salt and pepper. Add remaining potatoes. Drizzle with 1 tablespoon vinegar. Season with salt and pepper.

Melt butter in heavy large skillet over high heat. Add shrimp and scallops and sauté until cooked through, about 5 minutes. Transfer shrimp, scallops and any juices to bowl with potatoes; add crabmeat. Toss gently to blend. Cover and refrigerate until well chilled, about 2 hours. (*Can be prepared 1 day ahead. Keep refrigerated.*)

Stir sour cream, mayonnaise, green onions, minced tarragon and remaining 1 tablespoon vinegar in small bowl to blend. Pour dressing over potato mixture. Toss gently to blend. Season to taste with salt and pepper. Garnish with tarragon sprigs and serve.

ORANGE CHICKEN AND MIXED GREENS SALAD

Make this impressive dish the centerpiece of your buffet table.

10 SERVINGS

⅔ cup plus ¼ cup fresh orange juice
¼ cup honey
4 large garlic cloves, minced
1 tablespoon minced fresh thyme or 1 teaspoon dried
2 teaspoons grated orange peel
8 boneless chicken breast halves with skin
Salt and pepper

3 oranges, peel and white pith removed

6 tablespoons olive oil
¼ cup white wine vinegar
1 large shallot, minced
1 pound mixed greens
1 orange or yellow bell pepper, seeded, thinly sliced

Fresh thyme sprigs (optional)

Mix ⅔ cup orange juice, honey, 3 garlic cloves, minced thyme and orange peel in 13x9x2-inch glass baking dish. Add chicken breasts and turn to coat. Cover and chill overnight, turning occasionally.

Prepare barbecue (medium-high heat) or preheat broiler. Remove chicken from marinade; reserve marinade. Season chicken with salt and pepper. Grill chicken until cooked through, about 4 minutes per side. Transfer to plate.

Boil reserved marinade in heavy small saucepan until reduced to ¼ cup, about 10 minutes. Cut oranges between membranes to release segments. *(Chicken, reduced marinade and orange segments can be prepared 2 hours ahead. Cover separately and store at room temperature. Rewarm marinade before using.)*

Whisk oil, vinegar, shallot and remaining ¼ cup orange juice and garlic clove in small bowl to blend. Season dressing with salt and pepper. Combine greens, bell pepper and orange segments in very large bowl. Toss with dressing.

Arrange greens in center of large platter.

Cut chicken diagonally into ½-inch-thick slices. Overlap chicken slices around outside edge of platter. Drizzle chicken with marinade. Garnish with thyme sprigs, if desired.

THE DIRT ON GARLIC

Garlic's popularity continues to grow. Whether topping a pizza, flavoring roasted meats or spiking a pasta salad, the "stinking rose" has become the seasoning of choice. Garlic has also been credited with various healing powers—everything from reducing high blood pressure and cholesterol levels to preventing certain types of cancer. For fresh answers to garlicky questions, call the Garlic Information Center at 800-330-5922. The hot line is run by the New York Hospital-Cornell University Medical Center, which also offers a free brochure all about garlic.

SMOKED SALMON SALAD

If you can't find yellow pear or yellow cherry tomatoes, use all red cherry tomatoes.

4 SERVINGS

6 tablespoons olive oil
3 tablespoons balsamic vinegar
    Salt and pepper

6 cups baby greens
6 ounces thinly sliced smoked salmon
1½ tablespoons drained capers
½ small red onion, thinly sliced
16 red cherry tomatoes
16 yellow pear or cherry tomatoes

Whisk oil and vinegar in small bowl to blend well. Season with salt and pepper.

Place greens in large bowl. Toss with enough dressing to coat lightly. Divide greens among 4 plates. Arrange smoked salmon slices over greens on each plate, dividing equally. Drizzle more dressing over salmon. Sprinkle salmon with capers. Garnish salads with red onion and red and yellow tomatoes.

SMOKED TURKEY SALAD WITH BING CHERRIES AND HAZELNUTS

6 SERVINGS

1¼ pounds smoked turkey breast, diced
 1 cup chopped green onions
 ¾ cup chopped celery
 ⅓ cup low-fat mayonnaise
 3 tablespoons chopped fresh thyme
   Salt and pepper

 6 tablespoons olive oil
 3 tablespoons white wine vinegar

 8 ounces mixed baby greens
2⅓ cups coarsely chopped pitted Bing cherries
 ½ cup coarsely chopped husked toasted hazelnuts

Mix turkey, green onions, celery, ⅓ cup mayonnaise and 2 tablespoons chopped thyme in medium bowl. Season salad with salt and pepper.

Whisk oil, vinegar and remaining 1 tablespoon chopped thyme in small bowl to blend. Season with salt and pepper.

Toss greens and vinaigrette in large bowl. Divide among plates. Add cherries and nuts to turkey. Place atop greens.

SOUTHWESTERN GRILLED BEEF SALAD WITH CORN SALSA AND CHIPOTLE DRESSING

Cumin, chili powder, garlic and fresh lime juice are combined in the easy-to-make spice paste. It adds lots of flavor to the beef in this recipe, but can also be used on chicken, pork, shrimp or firm fish like halibut, swordfish and shark.

6 SERVINGS

DRESSING

 ¼ cup fresh lime juice
 ¼ cup chopped fresh cilantro
 1 tablespoon chopped canned chipotle chilies in adobo sauce*
 2 large garlic cloves, pressed
 1 cup olive oil

Salt and pepper

Whisk first 4 ingredients in medium bowl to blend. Gradually whisk in oil. Season with salt and pepper. (*Can be made 1 day ahead. Cover and refrigerate.*)

Available at Latin American markets, specialty foods stores and in the Latin section of some supermarkets.

SALSA

 2 ears fresh corn, husked
 4 plum tomatoes, seeded, chopped
 1 cup chopped peeled jicama
 ½ cup chopped red onion
 ¼ cup chopped fresh cilantro

Blanch corn in large pot of boiling salted water 2 minutes. Drain. Cool. Cut corn from cob. Transfer corn kernels to large bowl. Add tomatoes, jicama, onion and cilantro and mix. (*Can be prepared 6 hours ahead. Cover and chill.*)

STEAK

1½ tablespoons fresh lime juice
 1 tablespoon ground cumin
 1 tablespoon chili powder

3 large garlic cloves, pressed
2 pounds beef tenderloin steaks
  (1 inch thick)

Combine first 4 ingredients in small bowl. Spread spice paste over both sides of steaks. Cover and refrigerate at least 2 hours or up to 6 hours.

ASSEMBLY

1 avocado, halved, peeled, pitted, diced
10 cups mixed baby greens
2 small mangoes, peeled, pitted, thinly sliced

Prepare barbecue (medium-high heat). Grill steaks to desired doneness, about 5 minutes per side for medium-rare. Transfer steaks to cutting board and let stand 5 minutes.

Meanwhile, add avocado and 2 tablespoons dressing to salsa and mix. Season to taste with salt and pepper. Place greens in large bowl and toss with enough dressing to coat. Divide greens equally among 6 plates. Fan some mango slices on 1 side of each salad. Top each salad with ½ cup salsa.

Thinly slice steaks crosswise. Arrange atop greens. Serve, passing remaining dressing separately.

CHICKEN SALAD WITH LENTILS, PEAS AND MINT

The traditional chicken salad gets dressed up for an elegant entrée. This one is perfect for a bridal or baby shower or a weekend lunch on the patio. Pour iced tea, lemonade or a crisp Sauvignon Blanc.

4 SERVINGS

3 cups water
⅔ cup dried lentils
3 tablespoons fresh lemon juice
3 tablespoons plus 1 teaspoon olive oil

2 large skinless boneless chicken breast halves
2 teaspoons (generous) curry powder
Salt and pepper

⅔ cup canned low-salt chicken broth
1 cup cauliflower florets
¾ cup fresh or frozen peas

2 small tomatoes, seeded, diced
1¼ cups diced English hothouse cucumber
2 green onions, sliced
3 tablespoons sour cream
2 tablespoons chopped fresh mint

2 large bunches watercress, trimmed
1 Asian pear* or Bartlett pear, peeled, cored, diced
1 large tomato, cut into wedges
Fresh mint sprigs

Bring 3 cups water and lentils to boil in heavy medium saucepan. Reduce heat to medium-low, cover and simmer until lentils are tender but still retain shape, about 20 minutes. Drain well. Transfer lentils to large bowl. Mix in 1 tablespoon lemon juice and 1 tablespoon oil. Cover and refrigerate.

Rub chicken breasts on both sides

with curry powder. Season with salt and pepper. Heat 1 teaspoon olive oil in heavy large skillet over medium-high heat. Add chicken breasts to skillet and cook until golden brown and cooked through, about 5 minutes per side. Transfer chicken to plate and refrigerate until well chilled.

Add chicken broth to same skillet and bring to boil. Add cauliflower and peas and cook over high heat until vegetables are crisp-tender and most of liquid has evaporated, about 5 minutes. Add mixture to lentils.

Cut chicken into ½-inch cubes and add to lentils along with any accumulated juices. Mix in diced tomatoes, diced cucumber, sliced green onions, sour cream and chopped fresh mint. Season salad to taste with salt and pepper. Cover and refrigerate until well chilled, about 2 hours. (*Salad can be prepared 1 day ahead. Keep refrigerated.*)

Toss watercress with remaining 2 tablespoons lemon juice and 2 tablespoons oil. Season to taste with salt and pepper. Mix pear into chicken salad. Mound chicken salad in center of 4 plates. Surround with watercress. Garnish salad with tomato wedges and mint sprigs and serve.

Also called Chinese pear and apple pear. Available in the produce section of many supermarkets.

TUNA SALAD WITH OLIVES, ORANGE AND BELL PEPPER
A sophisticated, Spanish-style salad.

4 MAIN-COURSE SERVINGS

¼ cup olive oil
¼ cup red wine vinegar
1 tablespoon minced garlic
3 seedless oranges, peel and white pith removed
1 small red onion, halved, thinly sliced
1 red bell pepper, thinly sliced
1 9-ounce can white meat tuna packed in water, drained well, separated into chunks
¼ cup chopped pimiento-stuffed green olives
¼ cup chopped fresh parsley
Salt and pepper

8 cups mixed salad greens
⅓ cup slivered almonds, toasted

Whisk oil, vinegar and garlic in large bowl to blend. Working over bowl with dressing, cut oranges between membranes, releasing segments into bowl. Add onion, bell pepper, tuna, olives and parsley; toss. Season with salt and pepper. (*Can be made 2 hours ahead. Cover; refrigerate.*)

Divide salad greens among plates. Spoon tuna salad over, dividing equally. Garnish with almonds.

Couscous, Shrimp and Pea Salad with Saffron Vinaigrette

A colorful mix of tomatoes, peas and yellow bell peppers enhances this entrée.

6 SERVINGS

- ½ cup sherry wine vinegar
- 1 teaspoon saffron threads
- ¾ cup olive oil
- 2 shallots, peeled, thinly sliced
- 2 teaspoons ground coriander
- 2 teaspoons fennel seeds
  Salt and pepper

- 2 cups couscous
- 2¼ cups boiling water

- 1 cup shelled or frozen peas
- 1½ pounds medium-sized peeled cooked shrimp
- 1 yellow bell pepper, cut into matchstick-size strips
- 1 cup halved cherry tomatoes

Heat vinegar and saffron in heavy small saucepan over medium heat, stirring until saffron softens, about 3 minutes. Cool. Combine oil, shallots, coriander and fennel seeds in medium bowl. Gradually whisk in vinegar mixture. Season with salt and pepper. Cover; chill until ready to use.

Place couscous in large bowl. Pour boiling water over. Cover and let stand until water is absorbed, about 10 minutes. Fluff with fork. Cool.

Cook peas in boiling salted water 1 minute. Drain. Add peas, shrimp and bell pepper to couscous. Mix in enough vinaigrette to season salad to taste. *(Can be made 8 hours ahead. Cover; chill.)* Mound in bowl. Place tomatoes around salad. Serve cold or at room temperature.

Main Courses

The main courses on the pages that follow are superb examples of light, fresh and easy. Witness such recipes as Grilled Swordfish with Tomato-Orange Salsa, Honey-Citrus Chicken, Beef and Broccoli Stir-Fry, or Minced Lamb with Ginger, Hoisin and Green Onions. Still others, however, promise more robust eating. Yet, even such hearty specialties as Ham Jambalaya, Buckwheat Pasta Primavera, or Goat Cheese-stuffed Turkey Burgers exemplify today's lighter, fresher, easier approach to cooking.

Seafood

SALMON WITH SESAME-PEPPERCORN CRUST

4 SERVINGS

¼ cup sesame seeds
1 tablespoon four-peppercorn spice mix*
1 lemon, quartered
4 6- to 7-ounce skinless salmon fillets
  Dried dillweed
  Garlic powder
  Salt
2 tablespoons (¼ stick) butter

Preheat oven to 350°F. Lightly grease large baking sheet. Combine sesame seeds and peppercorn mix in sealable plastic bag. Crush with mallet. Squeeze juice from lemon quarters onto both sides of salmon. Season both sides of salmon with dillweed, garlic powder, peppercorn mixture and salt. Arrange salmon on prepared baking sheet. Dot with butter.

Bake until fish is cooked through, about 15 minutes. Transfer to plates.

*A blend of black, white, pink and green peppercorns that is available in the spice section of many supermarkets.

SEA BASS WITH MEXICANA-CHINOISE SAUCE

4 MAIN-COURSE SERVINGS

  Nonstick vegetable oil spray
1 large onion, chopped
6 garlic cloves, chopped
1 tablespoon chopped fresh ginger
1 fresh poblano chili* or other mild green chili, stemmed, seeded, cut into matchstick-size strips
8 mushrooms, thinly sliced
⅔ cup dry white wine
¼ cup soy sauce
2 tablespoons black bean garlic sauce (lee kum kee)**
1 tablespoon orange marmalade
1 tablespoon fresh lime juice
4 8-ounce sea bass fillets (about 1 inch thick)
  Salt and pepper
2 tablespoons chopped fresh cilantro

Spray large nonstick skillet with vegetable oil spray; place over medium-high heat. Add onion, garlic and ginger; sauté until golden, about 3 minutes. Add chili and mushrooms; sauté 1 minutes. Stir in wine, soy sauce, black bean sauce, marmalade and lime juice; bring to boil. Season fish with salt and pepper. Place in same skillet. Reduce heat to medium-low. Cover and simmer until fish is just cooked through, about 5 minutes per side.

Transfer fish to plates. Spoon sauce around. Sprinkle with cilantro.

*A fresh green chili, often called a pasilla, available at Latin American markets and some supermarkets.

**Available at Asian markets and in the Asian section of some supermarkets.

Grilled Swordfish with Tomato-Orange Salsa

No one will feel cheated when this low-calorie entrée comes to the table. It's colorful and delicious. Team it with some iced herbal tea, and serve lemon sorbet with blueberries for dessert.

6 SERVINGS

SALSA

3 oranges, peeled, white pith removed, seeded, diced
1½ cups chopped seeded tomatoes
¼ cup minced red onion
¼ cup chopped fresh parsley
2 tablespoons fresh orange juice
2 teaspoons minced garlic
2 teaspoons balsamic vinegar
1 teaspoon minced peeled fresh ginger
⅛ teaspoon cayenne pepper
Salt and pepper

MARINADE

¾ cup bottled teriyaki sauce
⅔ cup dry sherry
4 teaspoons minced garlic
2 teaspoons minced peeled fresh ginger
1 teaspoon Oriental sesame oil

6 5- to 6-ounce swordfish steaks (1 inch thick)

FOR SALSA: Toss all ingredients in large bowl. Season to taste with salt and pepper. Let stand at least 1 hour. (*Can be prepared 4 hours ahead. Cover and refrigerate. Bring to room temperature before using.*)

FOR MARINADE: Combine first 5 ingredients in small saucepan. Bring marinade to boil. Set aside to cool.

Place swordfish in single layer in shallow glass baking dish. Pour marinade over swordfish; turn to coat evenly. Cover and refrigerate fish 1½ hours, turning often.

Prepare barbecue (medium-high heat). Remove fish from marinade. Grill until opaque in center, about 4 minutes per side. Transfer to platter. Serve with salsa.

TWO-PEPPER SHRIMP

(COVER RECIPE)

Crushed red pepper and cracked black pepper give this delicious dish its heat.

4 SERVINGS

1 pound uncooked large shrimp, peeled, deveined
4 tablespoons dry white wine
2 teaspoons grated peeled fresh ginger
½ teaspoon cracked black pepper
¼ teaspoon dried crushed red pepper

8 tablespoons rice vinegar
2 cups plus 2 tablespoons cold water
5 cups shredded romaine lettuce
8 radishes, trimmed, thinly sliced

½ cup bottled clam juice
2 teaspoons cornstarch
½ teaspoon salt
¼ teaspoon sugar

4 teaspoons vegetable oil

1 pound onions, thinly sliced
½ cup drained canned diced tomatoes
1 garlic clove, minced
2 tablespoons chopped fresh parsley
Salt and pepper

Mix shrimp, 2 tablespoons wine, ginger, black pepper and crushed red pepper in large bowl. Cover and chill 30 minutes. Drain, reserving marinade.

Pour 7 tablespoons rice vinegar into another large bowl. Add 2 cups cold water to bowl. Add shredded lettuce and radishes. Let stand 5 minutes. Drain.

Whisk clam juice, remaining 2 tablespoons wine and remaining 1 tablespoon vinegar in medium bowl to blend. Add cornstarch, salt and sugar; whisk until cornstarch dissolves. Whisk in reserved shrimp marinade. Set aside.

Heat 2 teaspoons oil in large non-stick skillet over medium-high heat. Add shrimp and sauté until just cooked through, about 2 minutes. Using slot-ted spoon, transfer shrimp to plate. Heat remaining 2 teaspoons oil in same skillet over medium-high heat. Add onions and sauté until beginning to soften, about 4 minutes. Add remaining 2 tablespoons water and stir 1 minute. Add tomatoes and garlic and stir 30 seconds. Rewhisk clam juice mixture to blend. Add to skillet and boil until sauce thickens, about 1 minute. Add shrimp and parsley and toss to coat. Season to taste with salt and pepper. Remove from heat.

Divide lettuce and radishes among 4 plates. Spoon shrimp mixture and sauce over and serve.

SEAFOOD-STUFFED EGGPLANT

8 SERVINGS

4 medium eggplants (about 1
    pound each), split lengthwise
2 cups water
1 teaspoon salt

4 tablespoons vegetable oil
2 onions, chopped (about 2 cups)
1 pound uncooked large shrimp,
    peeled, deveined, coarsely
    chopped
¼ teaspoon cayenne pepper
1 cup plus 2 tablespoons dry
    Italian-style breadcrumbs
½ pound crabmeat, drained well,
    picked over
    Salt and pepper

Preheat broiler. Arrange eggplants on
large baking sheet. Pierce with fork.
Broil 4 minutes per side. Scoop out
eggplant pulp, leaving ½-inch-thick
shell intact. Place eggplant pulp in
heavy medium saucepan. Pour 2 cups
water over. Add 1 teaspoon salt. Bring
to boil. Reduce heat, cover and simmer 15 minutes. Uncover and simmer
until eggplant is very tender and liquid evaporates, about 5 minutes.
Remove from heat.

Preheat oven to 375°F. Brush eggplant shells with 1 tablespoon oil. Bake
until shells are tender but still hold
shape, about 20 minutes.

Meanwhile, heat 3 tablespoons oil
in heavy large skillet over medium-high
heat. Add onions; sauté until tender,
about 5 minutes. Add boiled eggplant,
shrimp and cayenne; sauté until shrimp
are cooked through, about 4 minutes.
Remove from heat. Stir in 1 cup breadcrumbs and crabmeat. Season with salt
and pepper. Fill eggplant shells with
seafood mixture. (*Can be prepared 1 day
ahead; refrigerate.*)

Preheat oven to 375°F. Sprinkle
stuffing with remaining 2 tablespoons
breadcrumbs. Bake stuffed eggplants
until heated through, about 30 minutes.
Let stand 5 minutes. Serve hot.

PACIFIC SALMON WITH ROASTED GARLIC

*Steam sugar snap peas and pour a
Chardonnay.*

8 SERVINGS

2 medium heads garlic, broken
    into separate cloves, peeled
½ cup (about) olive oil
3 tablespoons unsalted butter
    Salt and pepper

8 6- to 7-ounce salmon fillets
4 teaspoons fresh lemon juice

4 teaspoons chopped fresh rosemary

Preheat oven to 400°F. Place garlic in
ramekin. Pour enough oil over to
cover. Wrap ramekin in double thickness of foil. Bake until garlic is very tender, about 35 minutes. Using slotted
spoon, transfer garlic and 1 tablespoon
cooking oil to food processor. Add butter to processor; puree. Season with salt
and pepper.

Preheat oven to 450°F. Place

salmon on baking sheet. Season with salt and pepper. Drizzle each fillet with ½ teaspoon lemon juice, then spread 1 tablespoon garlic puree over each. (*Can be made 1 day ahead; chill.*)

Bake salmon uncovered until just cooked through, about 15 minutes. Sprinkle rosemary over and serve.

BAKED STRIPED SEA BASS WITH TOMATOES

Whole sea bass stuffed with cilantro and surrounded by cherry tomatoes make an impressive presentation. Pour a chilled Chardonnay throughout the meal.

8 SERVINGS

- ¾ cup plus 3 tablespoons olive oil
- 6 tablespoons balsamic vinegar
- 2 tablespoons chopped fresh cilantro
- 2 tablespoons chopped fresh basil or 2 teaspoons dried
- Salt and pepper
- 2 1-pint baskets cherry tomatoes, halved
- 3 2-pound whole striped bass, cleaned, heads and tails left intact
- 3 tablespoons fresh lemon juice
- 3 tablespoons coarse salt
- 2 bunches cilantro sprigs, trimmed
- 10 shallots, chopped

Whisk ¾ cup oil and vinegar in medium bowl to blend. Stir in chopped cilantro and basil. Season with salt and pepper. Mix tomatoes into dressing. (*Tomatoes can be made 2 hours ahead. Let stand at room temperature.*)

Preheat oven to 350°F. Place fish on large baking sheet. Rub inside of each fish with 1 tablespoon lemon juice and ½ tablespoon coarse salt. Stuff cavities with cilantro sprigs and shallots, dividing equally among fish. Sprinkle each fish with ½ tablespoon coarse salt, then 1 tablespoon olive oil.

Bake fish until just opaque in center, about 30 minutes. Transfer to large platter. Spoon tomato mixture around fish and serve.

CHOLESTEROL LOWDOWN

Some researchers claim that the unhealthful effects of cholesterol have been exaggerated, but a recent edition of *Consumer Reports on Health* states otherwise. The latest available data supports the finding that lowering dietary cholesterol could prevent heart disease and even reverse atherosclerosis by reducing plaque buildup in the arteries. Though drug therapy can help bring levels back under control, lifestyle choices are less costly and less extreme ways to improve health in this area: Eat a diet low in saturated fat and cholesterol, don't smoke, and try to exercise regularly.

Poultry

TUSCAN CHICKEN WITH WARM BEAN SALAD

4 SERVINGS

1 4- to 4½-pound chicken, cut into
   10 pieces (2 breasts, each halved;
   2 wings; 2 thighs; 2 drumsticks)
9 garlic cloves
1 teaspoon salt
⅓ cup fresh lemon juice
4 tablespoons olive oil
3 tablespoons chopped fresh
   rosemary or 3 teaspoons dried
2½ tablespoons grated lemon peel
½ teaspoon sugar
   Pepper

3 15-ounce cans cannellini (white
   kidney beans), rinsed, drained

Arrange chicken in 13x9x2-inch baking dish. Mince 5 garlic cloves; mix in 1 teaspoon salt. Rub garlic mixture into chicken. Mix lemon juice, 2 tablespoons oil, 2 tablespoons rosemary, lemon peel and sugar in small bowl. Pour over chicken. Season with pepper. Cover; chill up to 3 hours.

Preheat oven to 350°F. Place cannellini in large skillet. Chop remaining 4 garlic cloves and mix into cannellini with 2 tablespoons oil and 1 tablespoon rosemary. Season with salt and pepper.

Uncover chicken and bake until cooked through but still juicy, basting occasionally, about 40 minutes. Remove from oven. Preheat broiler. Broil chicken until just brown, about 4 minutes.

Meanwhile, stir bean salad over medium heat until heated through, about 8 minutes. Spoon salad onto platter. Top with chicken and pan juices.

CHICKEN WITH MUSHROOMS AND WHITE WINE

4 SERVINGS

4 boneless chicken breast halves, with skin
Salt and pepper
All-purpose flour
2 tablespoons vegetable oil
1¼ pounds mushrooms, sliced
4 large shallots, chopped
1½ tablespoons chopped fresh thyme or 1½ teaspoons dried
1½ tablespoons chopped fresh tarragon or 1½ teaspoons dried
1½ cups canned low-salt chicken broth
1 cup dry white wine

Sprinkle chicken with salt and pepper; dust with flour. Heat oil in heavy large skillet over medium-high heat. Add chicken; sauté until brown, about 4 minutes per side. Transfer to plate. Add mushrooms, shallots and herbs to skillet. Sauté until mushrooms are cooked through and juices are reduced to glaze, about 12 minutes.

Add broth and wine to skillet. Boil until reduced by half, about 8 minutes. Return chicken to skillet. Simmer until chicken is cooked through and liquid thickens to sauce consistency, about 6 minutes. Season with salt and pepper. Transfer chicken and sauce to plates.

CHICKEN WITH MILD RED CHILI SAUCE

8 SERVINGS

¾ cup fresh lemon juice
¾ cup dry white wine
6 tablespoons olive oil
4½ tablespoons California chili powder*
9 garlic cloves, chopped
3 shallots, chopped
2 tablespoons soy sauce
2 tablespoons honey
1½ tablespoons fresh oregano leaves or 1½ teaspoons dried
8 large boneless chicken breast halves with skin
Salt and pepper

Oregano sprigs (optional)

Puree first 9 ingredients in blender until smooth. Using meat mallet, pound chicken breasts between sheets of plastic wrap to ½-inch thickness. Place chicken in 13x9x2-inch glass baking dish. Pour marinade over and turn to coat. Cover and refrigerate overnight.

Prepare barbecue (medium-high heat) or preheat broiler. Drain marinade into small saucepan. Boil 5 minutes. Season chicken with salt and pepper.

Grill or broil chicken until cooked through, about 5 minutes per side. Brush some marinade over chicken. Transfer to platter. Garnish with oregano sprigs, if desired. Serve with remaining marinade.

*A mild red chili powder available in the spice section of some supermarkets. If unavailable, use regular mild chili powder.

Honey-Citrus Chicken

Don't let the name fool you. This chicken is sweet from the honey, but it's also very spicy from a jalapeño chili and plenty of black pepper. The chicken needs to marinate for at least four hours, so begin preparing it ahead of time.

8 SERVINGS

- 1 medium pineapple, peeled, cored, coarsely chopped
- 1 medium jalapeño chili, seeded, finely chopped
- 1 teaspoon minced garlic
- 1 cup orange juice
- ½ cup fresh lime juice
- 3 tablespoons soy sauce
- 2 tablespoons (packed) chopped fresh cilantro
- 2 tablespoons (packed) chopped fresh basil
- 1 tablespoon ground black pepper
- 1 teaspoon grated orange peel
- 1 teaspoon grated lime peel
- 8 large skinless boneless chicken breast halves

- 2 tablespoons honey
- 3 tablespoons butter
  Salt and pepper

  Fresh cilantro sprigs
  Fresh basil sprigs

Puree pineapple, jalapeño and garlic in blender until almost smooth. Pour pineapple puree into 13x9x2-inch glass dish. Add orange juice, lime juice, soy sauce, chopped cilantro, chopped basil, black pepper, orange peel and lime peel to puree. Stir to combine. Add chicken to marinade and turn to coat. Cover and refrigerate at least 4 hours, turning often. (*Can be made 1 day ahead. Keep chilled.*)

Remove chicken from marinade. Using rubber spatula, lightly scrape excess marinade from chicken. Strain marinade into heavy medium saucepan. Transfer ⅓ cup marinade to small bowl; whisk in honey. Boil remaining marinade until reduced to 1½ cups sauce, about 15 minutes. Whisk in butter. Season sauce to taste

with salt and pepper.

Prepare barbecue (medium-high heat). Brush grill with oil. Grill chicken until cooked through, turning and basting often with reserved honey marinade, about 10 minutes.

Transfer chicken to platter. Garnish with cilantro and basil sprigs. Serve, passing sauce separately.

Baked Chicken with Tangy Barbecue Sauce

For this robust and easy entrée, chicken is baked with a barbecue-style glaze. Removing the skin cuts back on fat.

6 TO 8 SERVINGS

- 1 cup all-purpose flour
- 1 tablespoon garlic powder
- 1 tablespoon onion powder
- 1 tablespoon poultry seasoning
- 2 4-pound chickens, each cut into 6 pieces
  Salt and pepper

¼ cup vegetable oil

½ cup finely chopped onion
2 large garlic cloves, minced
1 20-ounce bottle ketchup
3 tablespoons (packed) golden
  brown sugar
1 tablespoon Worcestershire sauce
1 tablespoon Dijon mustard

Preheat oven to 325°F. Mix first 4 ingredients in large bowl. Season chicken with salt and pepper. Drop chicken 2 pieces at a time into flour mixture; toss to coat.

Heat oil in heavy large Dutch oven over medium heat. Working in batches, add chicken to pot; fry until brown, about 5 minutes per side. Arrange chicken on baking sheet. Bake 20 minutes.

Meanwhile, pour off all but 1 tablespoon oil from pot. Add onion and garlic; sauté over medium heat 5 minutes. Add ketchup. Fill ketchup bottle with water; pour water into pot. Mix in sugar, Worcestershire sauce and

mustard. Boil sauce until slightly thickened, stirring occasionally, about 10 minutes.

Remove chicken from oven. Spoon some sauce over chicken. Return chicken to oven. Bake until chicken is cooked through and glazed, about 20 minutes. Serve chicken with remaining sauce.

CHICKEN AND BROCCOLI STIR-FRY

4 SERVINGS

¼ cup canned low-salt chicken broth
3 tablespoons soy sauce
2 tablespoons dry sherry
1 tablespoon cornstarch

4 skinless boneless chicken breast
  halves, cut crosswise into ½-inch-
  wide strips
  Salt and pepper
2 tablespoons vegetable oil
2 large garlic cloves, chopped
1 tablespoon chopped peeled fresh

ginger
2 cups broccoli florets
1 red bell pepper, thinly sliced
1 small onion, thinly sliced
  Large pinch of dried crushed red
  pepper (optional)
  Hot cooked white rice

Whisk chicken broth, soy sauce, sherry and cornstarch in small bowl until cornstarch dissolves.

Season chicken with salt and pepper. Heat vegetable oil in heavy large skillet over high heat. Add garlic and ginger and stir until fragrant, about 30 seconds. Add chicken to skillet and stir-fry until white, about 2 minutes. Add broccoli florets, bell pepper, onion and crushed red pepper, if desired, and stir-fry until vegetables are crisp-tender and chicken is just cooked through, about 3 minutes. Add chicken broth mixture and bring to boil, stirring constantly. Cook until sauce thickens, about 1 minute. Serve with rice.

POACHED CHICKEN WITH CURRIED YOGURT SAUCE

The Mango and Red Onion Salsa (see page 73) is nice alongside this low-fat entrée.

4 SERVINGS

1 cup plain low-fat yogurt
¼ cup fresh lime juice
2 teaspoons ground cumin
2 teaspoons curry powder
   Salt and pepper

4 skinless boneless chicken breast
   halves
2 cups (or more) canned low-salt
   chicken broth

Combine first 4 ingredients in small bowl; whisk to blend. Season with salt and pepper. (*Can be made 1 day ahead. Cover; chill. Bring to room temperature before serving.*)

Arrange chicken in single layer in heavy medium skillet. Add enough broth to cover chicken and bring broth to boil. Cover skillet and turn off heat.

Let stand until chicken is cooked through, about 20 minutes. Using tongs, transfer chicken to plates. Cut chicken crosswise into thin slices. Spoon yogurt sauce over chicken.

HERB-ROASTED CHICKEN

6 SERVINGS

2 pounds plum tomatoes, cut
   crosswise into ⅓-inch-thick
   rounds
3 bunches (about) fresh thyme
8 sprigs fresh rosemary
4 tablespoons olive oil
2 4-pound chickens, rinsed,
   patted dry
   Salt and pepper
2 cups canned low-salt chicken
   broth
¼ cup chopped fresh parsley

Preheat oven to 400°F. Arrange tomato slices in single layer on bottom of large roasting pan. Arrange half of thyme and half of rosemary sprigs over. Heat 2 tablespoons oil in heavy large Dutch oven over medium-high heat. Season chickens with salt and pepper. Add 1 chicken to pot and brown on all sides, about 10 minutes. Using tongs, place chicken atop tomatoes in roasting pan. Heat 2 tablespoons oil in same Dutch oven. Repeat browning with second chicken. Transfer to pan. Divide remaining thyme and rosemary sprigs between chicken cavities. Pour broth into pan. Sprinkle chickens with parsley. Cover pan tightly with heavy-duty foil.

Bake chickens until cooked through and juices run clear when thighs are pierced with knife, about 50 minutes. Place chickens on platter. Discard herb sprigs. Using slotted spoon, arrange tomatoes around chickens. Pour pan juices into measuring cup. Spoon off fat from top. Transfer juices to small bowl; serve with chicken.

ORANGE-BRANDY CHICKEN

This makes a nice entrée for a dinner party.

4 SERVINGS

2 tablespoons (¼ stick) butter
4 boneless chicken breast halves
1 teaspoon minced fresh rosemary
   or ½ teaspoon dried
   Salt and pepper
⅓ cup frozen orange juice
   concentrate, thawed
⅓ cup canned chicken broth
2 tablespoons brandy
   Orange slices (optional)

Melt butter in heavy large skillet over medium-high heat. Season chicken with rosemary, salt and pepper. Add chicken to skillet and sauté until brown, about 3 minutes per side. Add orange juice concentrate, chicken broth and brandy and simmer until chicken is just cooked through, about 5 minutes. Transfer chicken to plate; tent with foil to keep warm. Boil pan juices until thickened to sauce consistency, stirring occasionally, about 5 minutes. Spoon sauce over chicken. Garnish with orange slices, if desired, and serve.

THE SKINNY ON CHICKEN

In their continuing efforts to satisfy customers who are ever more health conscious, fast-food chains have begun offering roasted or rotisserie-broiled chicken as an alternative to fried. But, as the University of California at Berkeley Wellness Letter points out, the method of preparation doesn't really have a significant impact on your fat intake; what matters is the type of meat you order and what you do with the skin.

Although a roasted chicken breast with its skin does contain much less fat and fewer calories than one that is fried, it still derives over 30 percent of its calories from fat. And the difference between fried and roasted becomes negligible once the skin is peeled away; if you stick with white meat, the fried chicken (sans skin) has just slightly more fat and calories than the roasted bird and gets only about 22 percent of its calories from fat.

The bottom line is easy to remember: However chicken might be cooked, order only white meat and strip away the skin for the most healthful results.

Meat

STEAKS WITH HERB-SPICE BLEND

The versatile seasoning mixture is just as nice on lamb, pork and poultry.

4 SERVINGS

1 tablespoon ground black pepper
1 tablespoon ground white pepper
1 tablespoon salt
1½ teaspoons celery seeds
1½ teaspoons dried thyme
1½ teaspoons dill seeds
1½ teaspoons mustard seeds
1½ teaspoons garlic powder
½ teaspoon dried crushed red pepper

4 1-inch-thick beef tenderloin steaks

Combine first 9 ingredients in blender and chop finely. Transfer to small container. (*Can be prepared 2 months ahead. Cover tightly and store in refrigerator.*)

Prepare barbecue (medium-high heat) or preheat broiler. Sprinkle ½ teaspoon herb-spice blend on each side of each steak. Grill or broil steaks to desired doneness, about 3 minutes per side for medium-rare.

BEEF AND BROCCOLI STIR-FRY

4 SERVINGS

¼ cup soy sauce
¼ cup dry sherry
1 tablespoon honey
1 tablespoon (packed) chopped garlic
2 teaspoons grated orange peel
1 pound flank steak, cut diagonally across grain into thin strips

1 large head broccoli, cut into florets

2 tablespoons vegetable oil
1 tablespoon cornstarch
Salt and pepper
Cooked white rice

Whisk first 5 ingredients in large bowl.

Add meat; toss to coat. Cover and refrigerate at least 1 hour and up to 4 hours.

Blanch broccoli in large pot of boiling salted water 2 minutes. Drain. Rinse under cold water; drain well.

Heat oil in heavy large wok or skillet over high heat. Drain meat well, reserving marinade. Add cornstarch to reserved marinade and mix until smooth; set aside. Add meat to wok and stir-fry until almost cooked through, about 2 minutes. Add broccoli and stir-fry until crisp-tender, about 2 minutes. Add reserved marinade mixture and boil until sauce thickens and coats meat and broccoli, stirring constantly, about 2 minutes. Season to taste with salt and pepper. Serve over rice.

NEW LABELS FOR MEAT

No longer is there any reason to be confused about the proper way to handle meats. That's because a new U.S. Department of Agriculture rule requires that safe-handling information be included right on the package. The rule went into effect last fall for ground meat and poultry products and this past April for all other meats.

If you're not much of a label reader, here are the basic guidelines: Keep meats refrigerated, or freeze for later use; if frozen, thaw them in the refrigerator or microwave. Keep raw meat and poultry separate from other foods, and be sure to wash work surfaces, utensils and your hands after contact with raw meat. Cook meat and poultry thoroughly (many labels provide specific cooking temperatures), keep hot foods hot and refrigerate leftovers immediately.

GRILLED MARINATED LEG OF LAMB WITH KIWIFRUIT-MINT SALSA

Ask your butcher to butterfly the lamb for you.

8 SERVINGS

¼ cup olive oil
¼ cup chopped fresh rosemary or 1 tablespoon dried
¼ cup chopped fresh mint
4 garlic cloves, minced
2 teaspoons ground pepper
1½ cups dry red wine
½ cup red wine vinegar
1 5-pound leg of lamb, boned, butterflied

Kiwifruit-Mint Salsa (see recipe)

Process first 5 ingredients in processor until well blended. Add wine and vinegar and blend well. Place lamb, skin side down, in glass baking dish. Pour marinade over. Cover; chill at least 4 hours and up to 8 hours, turning occasionally.

Prepare barbecue (medium-high heat). Grill lamb to desired doneness, about 13 minutes per side for medium-rare. Place lamb on platter. Let stand 10 minutes. (*Can be prepared 2 hours ahead. Cover and let stand at room temperature.*) Slice lamb. Serve with salsa.

KIWIFRUIT-MINT SALSA

MAKES ABOUT 3 CUPS

9 kiwifruit, peeled, cut into ½-inch pieces
3 tablespoons finely chopped fresh mint leaves
2 tablespoons honey
1½ teaspoons chopped fresh rosemary

Mix all ingredients in bowl. (*Can be made 4 hours ahead. Cover and chill.*)

Marinated Pork and Red Onion Kebabs

The marinade for the pork is also excellent on lamb. Serve the kebabs with some rice to round out the meal.

4 SERVINGS

1½ pounds pork tenderloin, cut into 16 equal pieces
1 red onion, cut into 16 equal pieces
8 8- to 10-inch bamboo skewers, soaked in water 10 minutes
Salt and pepper

⅓ cup vegetable oil
¼ cup dry red wine
3 tablespoons red wine vinegar
3 tablespoons soy sauce
1 tablespoon chopped garlic
1 tablespoon chopped peeled fresh ginger
1½ teaspoons sugar

Thread 2 pieces of pork and 2 pieces of onion alternately on each skewer. Season with salt and pepper. Arrange kebabs in 13x9x2-inch glass baking dish.

Whisk all remaining ingredients in medium bowl. Pour marinade over kebabs. Let stand up to 2 hours at room temperature or cover and refrigerate up to 1 day, turning occasionally.

Preheat broiler. Drain marinade into small saucepan. Boil marinade 2 minutes. Broil kebabs until pork is cooked through, turning frequently and basting occasionally with marinade, about 12 minutes.

Sauté of Peppers, Onion, Spinach and Lamb

Strips of succulent lamb are added to a colorful vegetable trio in this easy and elegant main course. Accompany with crusty bread.

4 SERVINGS

2 tablespoons olive oil
½ pound lamb-leg cutlets or ½-inch-thick slices boneless leg of lamb, cut crosswise into ¼-inch-thick strips
Salt and pepper
2 red bell peppers, cut into ¼-inch-thick strips
1 large onion, sliced
3 garlic cloves, minced
¼ teaspoon dried crushed red pepper
1 10-ounce package ready-to-use fresh spinach
⅓ cup canned beef broth

Heat oil in heavy large skillet over high heat. Sprinkle lamb with salt and pepper. Add to skillet and sauté until lamb is brown on outside but still rare, about 2 minutes. Transfer to plate. Reduce heat to medium-high. Add bell peppers, onion and garlic to skillet; sauté until beginning to soften, about 5 minutes. Add crushed red pepper; sauté 30 seconds. Add spinach 1 handful at a time; toss until wilted after each addition. Season with salt and pepper. Return lamb and any collected juices to skillet; stir to heat through. Transfer to serving platter. Add beef broth to skillet and boil until syrupy, scraping up browned bits, about 2 minutes. Pour sauce over lamb and vegetables and serve.

MEDALLIONS OF PORK WITH PEAR SAUCE

Ready in under ten minutes, this sauce turns basic pork chops into an entrée good enough for company. Partner it with sautéed cabbage and roasted potatoes.

4 SERVINGS

2 tablespoons vegetable oil
4 ½-inch-thick boneless pork loin chops
   Dried rubbed sage
   Salt and pepper
   All-purpose flour

2 pears, peeled, cored, thinly sliced (about 1 pound)
⅓ cup dry white wine
2 tablespoons sugar
2 tablespoons chopped crystallized ginger

Heat oil in heavy large skillet over medium heat. Season pork with dried sage, salt and pepper. Coat pork with flour; shake off excess. Add pork to skillet and sauté until brown, about 3 minutes per side. Transfer to platter.

Drain fat from skillet. Add pears and sauté over medium heat 2 minutes. Stir in wine, sugar and ginger, scraping up any browned bits. Increase heat to high and boil until pears are tender and syrup is thick, about 5 minutes. Return pork and any accumulated juices to skillet. Simmer just until cooked through, about 1 minute. Season to taste with salt and pepper. Arrange pork on plates. Spoon sauce over and serve.

HAM JAMBALAYA

This quick one-pot meal is especially good with garlic toast or corn bread.

6 SERVINGS

3 tablespoons olive oil
2 large onions, diced
1 red bell pepper, diced
1 green bell pepper, diced
3 large garlic cloves, chopped
1 28-ounce can ready-cut tomatoes
2 cups diced ham
½ cup dry white wine
1 teaspoon dried thyme
1 teaspoon dried basil
1 teaspoon paprika
½ teaspoon cayenne pepper
¾ cup long-grain white rice
  Salt and pepper

Heat oil in large Dutch oven over medium heat. Add onions, bell peppers and garlic; sauté until beginning to soften, about 10 minutes. Mix in tomatoes with their juices, ham, wine, thyme, basil, paprika and cayenne pepper. Bring to boil. Gradually stir in rice.

Cover pot. Reduce heat to medium-low; simmer until rice is tender and most liquids are absorbed, about 25 minutes. Season with salt and pepper.

MINCED LAMB WITH GINGER, HOISIN AND GREEN ONIONS

Serve this quick stir-fry with rice.

4 SERVINGS

2 tablespoons orange juice
1 tablespoon cornstarch
1 pound ground lamb
1 tablespoon Oriental sesame oil
2 tablespoons minced peeled fresh ginger
1 tablespoon minced fresh garlic
1 tablespoon minced orange peel
1 bunch green onions, chopped
¼ cup hoisin sauce*
  Butter lettuce leaves

Combine orange juice and cornstarch in small bowl. Sauté lamb in heavy large skillet over high heat until cooked through, breaking up with back of spoon, about 5 minutes. Pour lamb with its juices into colander; drain. Heat oil in same skillet over high heat. Add ginger, garlic and orange peel; stir-fry 30 seconds. Add green onions and stir-fry 1 minute. Add hoisin sauce and lamb to skillet; stir until blended. Add orange juice mixture; stir until thickened, about 1 minute. Spoon into lettuce leaves.

Available at Asian markets and in the Asian section of some supermarkets.

GRILLED PORK CHOPS WITH CHERRY RELISH

The relish is also a delicious complement to grilled lamb or chicken.

4 SERVINGS

4 pork loin chops (each about
  ½ inch thick)
  Pepper
¼ cup low-sodium soy sauce

1 teaspoon vegetable oil
½ cup chopped onion
1 tablespoon chopped peeled

fresh ginger
1 teaspoon minced garlic
1 cup coarsely chopped pitted
  sweet cherries
  Salt

Season pork lightly with pepper. Place in shallow baking dish. Pour soy sauce over. Turn chops to coat. Cover; chill 1 hour, turning occasionally.

Heat oil in small skillet over medium heat. Add onion, ginger and garlic; sauté until onion is almost tender, about 5 minutes. Add cherries; sauté until cherries begin to soften, about 8 minutes. Remove from heat. Season with salt.

Prepare barbecue (medium-high heat) or preheat broiler. Remove pork from marinade. Grill pork until cooked through, about 4 minutes per side. Transfer to plates. Spoon relish over.

Vegetarian & Dairy

MUSHROOMS STROGANOFF

The low-fat mushroom ragout can also be served over toast points or as a side dish.

4 SERVINGS

1 tablespoon butter
2 large garlic cloves, chopped
1 large onion, thinly sliced
2 pounds mushrooms, sliced
1 tablespoon all-purpose flour
½ cup dry white wine
1 cup nonfat sour cream
¼ teaspoon ground nutmeg
  Salt and pepper
12 ounces linguine, freshly cooked

Melt butter in heavy large Dutch oven over medium-high heat. Add garlic and sauté 30 seconds. Add onion and sauté 2 minutes. Add mushrooms and sauté until tender and most liquid in pot evaporates, about 10 minutes. Reduce heat to medium. Add flour and stir 1 minute. Add white wine and cook until mixture thickens, stirring frequently, about 3 minutes. Mix in sour cream, then nutmeg. Season mushroom mixture to taste with salt and pepper. Add linguine to pot; toss to blend well and serve.

WHERE'S THE BEEF?

For vegetarians (or anyone) who might want the savory flavor of sausage without the meat, Fantastic Foods has a hearty and wholesome alternative. Nature's Sausage is made of grains, legumes and vegetables, with a mere 1.5 grams of fat and only 65 calories per serving. Perhaps the best news is that the product contains no saturated fat or cholesterol. Like the real stuff, Nature's Sausage is a good source of protein and can embellish any casserole or pizza with enough taste to satisfy even non-vegetarians.

White Bean, Butternut Squash, Kale and Olive Stew

Vegetable stews have made their way into many culinary repertoires. Aside from their obvious healthful qualities, they're easy to whip up at the last minute with whatever you may have on hand.

6 SERVINGS

¼ cup olive oil

3 large onions, chopped

6 garlic cloves, minced

1 3¼- to 3½-pound butternut squash, peeled, seeded, cut into 1½-inch cubes

3 red bell peppers, seeded, cut into 1½-inch pieces

1½ cups canned vegetable broth

1½ large bunches kale, thick stems trimmed, leaves cut crosswise into 2-inch strips

1 tablespoon dried rubbed sage

5 15-ounce cans cannellini (white kidney beans), rinsed, drained

1 cup Kalamata olives,* pitted, halved

Salt and pepper

Freshly grated Romano cheese

Heat oil in heavy large Dutch oven over medium-high heat. Add onions and garlic; sauté until tender, about 10 minutes. Add squash; sauté 10 minutes. Add bell peppers and stir to coat with onion mixture. Add broth. Cover and simmer until squash is just tender, about 10 minutes.

Mix kale and sage into stew. Cover and cook until kale wilts, stirring occasionally, about 8 minutes. Add beans and olives and stir until heated through. Season to taste with salt and pepper.

Transfer stew to large shallow bowl. Sprinkle generously with cheese.

*Kalamata olives are sold at Greek and Italian markets and some supermarkets.

GUT CHECK

If your love of rich or spicy cuisine is, unfortunately, paired with some common digestive problems, take heart. *Be Good to Your Gut* (Blackwell Science, 1995, $14.95) can help alleviate chronic ailments or the occasional upsets, like heartburn, that are associated with some foods. Pat Baird, a registered dietitian and nutrition consultant, gives practical advice for making smart dining choices away from home, as well as information about what might help specific problems. Each chapter explains the probable causes for a particular condition and offers several recipes for sensitive stomachs.

Pinto Bean and Feta Cheese Quesadillas

A fat-free spicy bean mixture and a sprinkling of low-fat, high-flavor feta cheese are sandwiched between whole wheat tortillas for quesadillas that even health-conscious eaters can enjoy. Rich in carbohydrates, this dish provides lots of energy.

8 SERVINGS

1½ 15- to 16-ounce cans pinto beans, drained, rinsed
¾ cup chopped red onion
¾ cup chopped fresh parsley
1½ jalapeño chilies, seeded, minced
1½ teaspoons chili powder
½ teaspoon ground cumin
    Salt and pepper

8 whole wheat flour tortillas (about 8-inch diameter)
8 tablespoons crumbled feta cheese (about 4 ounces)
    Vegetable oil

Combine first 6 ingredients in processor. Using on/off turns, process until very chunky puree forms. Transfer to bowl. Season with salt and pepper. *(Can be prepared 1 day ahead. Cover and chill.)*

Place 1 tortilla on work surface. Spread with ¼ of bean mixture. Top with 2 tablespoons cheese, then another tortilla. Heat heavy medium skillet over medium heat. Brush with oil. Add quesadilla; cook until beans are heated and tortillas are brown, about 4 minutes per side. Transfer to warm plate and cover to keep warm. Repeat with remaining tortillas, bean mixture and cheese. Cut each quesadilla into 8 wedges and serve.

USING YOUR BEAN

Almost all beans are low in fat (only about 2 to 5 percent of their calories come from fat) and high in complex carbohydrates, fiber and protein. In short, they're a great everyday food.

Brooke Dojny, a "30-Minute Main Courses" columnist of *Bon Appétit*, has compiled 75 of her best bean recipes for a new book, *Full of Beans* (HarperPerennial, 1996, $12.50). Dojny shows how versatile these legumes are, with recipes for bean soups, salads, tostadas and meatless main dishes. She includes a section on storage and cooking and even answers the historic question: to soak or not to soak.

COTTAGE CHEESE PANCAKES

These wholesome flapjacks are filled with the energy-boosting carbohydrates found in whole wheat flour and multigrain oatmeal. The fat is kept down by using low-fat cottage cheese, only two egg yolks and just two tablespoons of milk. To cook the pancakes, make sure to use a nonstick skillet brushed lightly with oil. Top them with the Peach and Berry Salad, and serve with reduced-fat sausages.

4 SERVINGS

1 pound low-fat cottage cheese
⅔ cup whole wheat flour
⅓ cup multigrain oatmeal
2 egg yolks
3 tablespoons honey
2 tablespoons milk
½ teaspoon vanilla extract
¼ teaspoon ground cardamom
6 egg whites

Vegetable oil
Peach and Berry Salad
(see recipe)

Mix cottage cheese, flour, oatmeal, egg yolks, honey, milk, vanilla and cardamom in large bowl. Beat whites in another large bowl until stiff but not dry. Fold whites into cottage cheese mixture in 2 additions.

Preheat oven to 200°F. Heat large nonstick skillet over medium heat. Brush with oil. Spoon batter onto skillet by ⅓ cupfuls, forming 4-inch-diameter pancakes. Cook pancakes until bottoms are brown and bubbles form on top, about 3 minutes. Turn; cook until bottoms are brown and pancakes are cooked through, about 4 minutes. Transfer to plate and place in oven to keep warm. Repeat with remaining batter. Serve immediately; pass Peach and Berry Salad to spoon over pancakes.

PEACH AND BERRY SALAD

You won't miss butter and syrup when this honey-sweetened fruit treat tops the pancakes. It's also delicious with waffles, French toast or on its own.

4 SERVINGS

3 peaches
2 ½-pint baskets blackberries
1 1-pint basket strawberries, hulled, sliced
¼ cup honey
½ teaspoon ground cardamom

Bring medium pot of water to boil. Add peaches and blanch 30 seconds. Drain. Transfer to medium bowl, cover with cold water and cool. Drain. Peel peaches and slice. Place in medium bowl. Add all remaining ingredients and mix to blend. (*Can be prepared 1 hour ahead. Cover and let stand at room temperature.*)

Pasta

Pasta with Mushrooms, Sun-dried Tomatoes and Pine Nuts

For a richer dish, you could splurge by adding an ounce of reconstituted dried porcini mushrooms to the sauce.

4 SERVINGS

12 sun-dried tomatoes
   (not oil-packed)
2 cups boiling water

Nonstick vegetable oil spray
1 pound mushrooms, thickly sliced
1 large onion, chopped
1 cup dry white wine
2 large garlic cloves, chopped

12 ounces penne

½ cup grated Parmesan cheese
¼ cup pine nuts, toasted
¼ cup sliced fresh basil or
   2 teaspoons dried
Salt and pepper

Place sun-dried tomatoes in small bowl. Pour 2 cups boiling water over. Let stand until tomatoes soften, about 15 minutes. Drain tomatoes, reserving soaking liquid. Thinly slice tomatoes.

Spray large nonstick skillet generously with vegetable oil spray. Add mushrooms, onion, wine, garlic, reserved tomato soaking liquid and sliced tomatoes. Bring to boil over high heat. Reduce heat to medium and simmer until liquids are reduced by half and vegetables are tender, about 25 minutes.

Meanwhile, cook pasta in large pot of boiling salted water until just tender but still firm to bite. Drain pasta, reserving 1 cup cooking liquid. Return pasta to same large pot.

Pour sauce from skillet over pasta. Add Parmesan cheese and pine nuts. Toss, adding reserved cooking liquid by ¼ cupfuls if mixture is dry. Mix in basil. Season to taste with salt and pepper.

LINGUINE WITH CLAMS AND WILD MUSHROOMS

Accompany this irresistible pasta dish with breadsticks and a dry white wine.

4 SERVINGS

6 tablespoons olive oil
1 pound mixed fresh wild
  mushrooms (such as oyster
  mushrooms and shiitake,
  stems trimmed, caps sliced)
6 large garlic cloves, minced
¼ teaspoon dried crushed red
  pepper
1 cup dry white wine
5 pounds clams (about 24
  littleneck)

1 pound linguine
  Salt and pepper

2 bunches fresh chives or 1 bunch
  green onions, chopped

Heat 3 tablespoons oil in heavy large Dutch oven over high heat. Add mushrooms and sauté until beginning to brown, about 5 minutes. Using slotted spoon, transfer mushrooms to plate. Add remaining 3 tablespoons oil and garlic to Dutch oven. Sauté until garlic is tender, about 3 minutes. Add crushed red pepper, then wine and clams. Cover and cook until clams open, about 8 minutes.

Meanwhile, cook linguine in large pot of boiling salted water until just tender but still firm to bite.

Drain pasta well and transfer to large bowl. Spoon mushrooms over, then top with clam mixture, discarding any clams that do not open. Season to taste with salt and pepper. Sprinkle with chives.

PASTA WITH RICOTTA AND FRESH HERBS

4 SERVINGS

1 15-ounce container low-fat ricotta
  cheese
⅔ cup nonfat milk
½ cup grated Parmesan cheese
2 teaspoons olive oil
1 cup chopped onion
2 garlic cloves, chopped
½ cup chopped fresh basil
¼ cup chopped fresh chives or
  green onions
¼ cup chopped fresh parsley
12 ounces rotelle or fusilli pasta,
  freshly cooked
  Salt and pepper

Blend ricotta cheese, milk and Parmesan in processor until smooth. Heat oil in heavy large skillet over medium heat. Add onion; sauté until beginning to brown, about 5 minutes. Add garlic and sauté 2 minutes. Add ricotta mixture, basil, chives and parsley to skillet; stir until heated through, about 5 minutes. Mix in rotelle. Season with salt and pepper.

FETTUCCINE WITH SHRIMP, TOMATOES AND ARTICHOKE HEARTS

6 SERVINGS

2 tablespoons olive oil
1/3 cup chopped onion
1/3 cup finely chopped carrot
1/3 cup finely chopped celery
4 teaspoons minced garlic
6 tablespoons all-purpose flour
1 28-ounce can Italian plum tomatoes, drained, coarsely chopped
1 16-ounce can Italian plum tomatoes, drained, coarsely chopped
4 cups canned low-salt chicken broth
1 cup dry white wine
2 1/4 teaspoons dried basil
1/4 teaspoon dried crushed red pepper
1 9-ounce package frozen artichoke hearts, thawed

1 1/4 pounds fettuccine
2 1/4 pounds uncooked large shrimp, peeled, deveined
Salt and pepper

6 tablespoons sliced fresh basil leaves
6 ounces Parmesan cheese, shaved with vegetable peeler into strips

Heat 2 tablespoons olive oil in heavy large Dutch oven over medium-high heat. Add chopped onion, chopped carrot and chopped celery and sauté vegetables 2 minutes. Add garlic and sauté 1 more minute. Sprinkle 6 tablespoons flour over vegetables and stir 2 minutes. Stir in all chopped canned tomatoes, chicken broth, dry white wine, dried basil and dried red pepper and bring to boil. Reduce heat to medium and cook until thickened to thin sauce consistency, stirring frequently, about 45 minutes. Add artichoke hearts and cook until tender, stirring occasionally, about 8 minutes. (*Sauce can be prepared 1 day ahead.*

Cover tightly and refrigerate.)

Cook pasta in pot of boiling salted water until tender but still firm to bite.

Meanwhile, bring tomato and artichoke sauce to simmer. Add 2¼ pounds shrimp to sauce; simmer until shrimp are cooked through, stirring sauce occasionally, about 5 minutes. Season sauce to taste with salt and pepper.

Drain pasta and divide among 6 plates. Spoon tomato and shrimp mixture over pasta. Sprinkle with sliced fresh basil leaves and Parmesan shavings and serve.

BUCKWHEAT PASTA PRIMAVERA

Buckwheat noodles give this classic spring pasta dish a nifty twist. Uncork your favorite Chardonnay.

4 SERVINGS

2½ cups canned low-salt chicken
    broth or water
1 ounce dried shiitake mushrooms
12 sun-dried tomatoes (not packed
    in oil; about 1 ounce)
1 large carrot, peeled, cut into
    matchstick-size strips (about
    1½ cups)
8 ounces sugar snap peas, trimmed

2 tablespoons (¼ stick) butter
1 large onion, sliced
1 yellow bell pepper, cut into strips
4 garlic cloves, minced
¼ cup whipping cream
    Salt and pepper

12 ounces dried buckwheat pasta
    (fancy soba)*
1 cup freshly grated Parmesan
    cheese
2 green onions, sliced
    Additional freshly grated
    Parmesan cheese

Bring broth to simmer in heavy medium saucepan. Rinse mushrooms briefly under cold water. Add mushrooms and sun-dried tomatoes to broth; simmer until tender, about 4 minutes. Using slotted spoon, transfer mushrooms and tomatoes to plate; cool. Add carrot and sugar snap peas to broth and cook until crisp-tender, about 3 minutes. Using slotted spoon, transfer vegetables to another plate. Boil broth remaining in saucepan until reduced to ¼ cup, about 5 minutes. Reserve broth. Discard mushroom stems. Slice mushroom caps and tomatoes.

Melt butter in heavy large skillet over medium-high heat. Add onion; sauté until tender and golden, about 8 minutes. Add bell pepper and garlic; stir until bell pepper is tender, about 4 minutes. Add carrot, sugar snap peas, mushrooms, sun-dried tomatoes, reserved broth and cream to skillet and bring to boil. Season with salt and pepper.

Meanwhile, cook pasta in large pot of boiling salted water until tender but still firm to bite, about 4 minutes. Drain. Place pasta in large bowl. Pour vegetables and sauce over pasta. Sprinkle with 1 cup Parmesan; toss to coat. Garnish with green onions. Serve, passing additional Parmesan separately.

Dried buckwheat pasta is available at Asian markets and in the Asian section of many supermarkets.

GOOD FOR PASTA

For the health-conscious, the new tomato sauces from Muir Glen are appealing—very appealing. The company has introduced three flavors that are fat-free and organic. These qualities sound even better with the encouraging (yet early) news that tomatoes may help to prevent some types of cancer.

But besides all that health stuff, taste is still the best indicator of a great sauce. And Muir Glen's Sun Dried Tomato, Cabernet Marinara and Garlic-Roasted Garlic sauces have delicious, robust flavor. Look for the sauces in grocery stores and natural foods stores nationwide.

PASTA WITH HERBED TURKEY SAUCE

4 SERVINGS

- 2 tablespoons olive oil
- 4 large garlic cloves, chopped
- 1 pound ground turkey
- 1 28-ounce can crushed tomatoes with added puree
- ½ cup dry white wine
- ½ cup chopped fresh parsley
- ½ cup chopped fresh basil or 1½ tablespoons dried
- 4 teaspoons chopped fresh oregano or 2 teaspoons dried
  Salt and pepper
- 12 ounces penne, freshly cooked

Heat olive oil in heavy large Dutch oven over medium-high heat. Add chopped garlic and sauté until tender, about 3 minutes. Add ground turkey and sauté until beginning to brown, breaking up large chunks with spoon, about 8 minutes. Add crushed tomatoes with puree, white wine, parsley, basil and oregano.

Reduce heat to medium-low and simmer mixture until thickened to sauce consistency, about 30 minutes. Season sauce to taste with salt and pepper. Add pasta to sauce and toss to combine.

FAST INFORMATION

Eating out more? Many people are—an average of four times a week, and mostly at fast-food establishments. That can take quite a toll on your health by adding large amounts of fat, cholesterol and sodium to your diet. *The Fast-Food Nutrition Counter* (Pocket Books, 1994, $5.99) can help you quickly navigate the endless menu selections to locate the most healthful eat-on-the-run entrées. This nifty paperback lists nutritional data on thousands of burgers, salads, tacos and other items from your favorite quick-stop and family-style joints, including McDonald's, Ponderosa, Red Lobster, TCBY and Sonic Drive-In.

Sandwiches

GOAT CHEESE-STUFFED TURKEY BURGERS WITH ROASTED RED PEPPER RELISH

The goat cheese and relish keep these burgers especially moist. For a nice variation, omit the goat cheese, and top the turkey burgers with sliced Havarti or Monterey Jack cheese during the last few minutes of cooking. Set out bowls of pickles and olives, and pour chilled Chardonnay throughout the meal.

6 SERVINGS

1½ pounds lean ground turkey
6 tablespoons fresh breadcrumbs
3 tablespoons fresh lemon juice
2 teaspoons grated lemon peel
2 teaspoons dried thyme
1⅛ teaspoons salt
½ teaspoon ground black pepper
6 tablespoons soft fresh goat cheese
(such as Montrachet)

6 whole wheat hamburger buns
Roasted Red Pepper Relish
(see recipe)

Combine turkey, breadcrumbs, lemon juice, lemon peel, thyme, salt and pepper in large bowl. Mix well. Divide turkey mixture into 6 equal portions. Form 1 portion into two 4-inch-diameter patties. Place 1 tablespoon goat cheese atop 1 turkey patty; place second patty atop cheese. Seal patties at edges to enclose cheese. Repeat with remaining 5 portions. *(Can be prepared 4 hours ahead. Cover and refrigerate.)*

Prepare barbecue (medium-high heat). Grill burgers until cooked through, about 5 minutes per side. Grill hamburger buns, cut side down, until lightly toasted, about 1 minute. Place turkey burgers on bottom half of buns. Top burgers with Roasted Red Pepper Relish, then bun tops and serve.

HOLD THE MAYO

Calling all sandwich lovers: Now there is a truly delicious way to get all the flavor of mayonnaise with less fat and cholesterol and fewer calories than the regular stuff has. Earth Island, a natural foods company in Canoga Park, California, has developed Vegenaise, an all-natural sandwich spread that doesn't use eggs or dairy products. The company also makes a variety with grape-seed oil, which is thought to raise the level of good blood cholesterol (HDL) and lower that of the bad (LDL). Look for Vegenaise in health food stores and specialty foods stores, or call 818-347-9946 for more information.

Roasted Red Pepper Relish

Purchased roasted sweet red peppers, available in jars, make this snappy relish very easy to prepare.

MAKES ABOUT 2 CUPS

3 tablespoons olive oil
4 7-ounce jars roasted sweet red peppers, rinsed, drained, patted dry, chopped
1½ cups chopped onions
3 teaspoons finely chopped garlic

4½ tablespoons cider vinegar
3 tablespoons sugar
¼ teaspoon dry mustard
¼ teaspoon cayenne pepper
Salt

Heat oil in heavy large skillet over medium-high heat. Add red peppers and sauté 2 minutes. Add onions and garlic. Cook until onions are tender, stirring frequently, about 5 minutes.

Mix vinegar and sugar in small bowl until sugar dissolves. Stir vinegar mixture into red peppers. Mix in mustard and cayenne pepper. Season with salt. Continue cooking relish until all liquid has evaporated, stirring frequently, about 6 minutes. Cool to room temperature. *(Can be prepared 1 day ahead. Cover and refrigerate. Bring to room temperature before using.)*

CONSIDERING CARBS

Americans are now eating less-fatty foods. That's good. However, Americans are still eating high-calorie foods. That's bad. The result: While overall fat intake has decreased, body weights are still going up. Dr. Scott Grundy is the director of the Center for Human Nutrition at the University of Texas Southwestern Medical Center in Dallas, and he thinks the problem lies with a person's daily intake of calories from carbohydrates found abundantly in starchy foods like breads and pasta. According to Grundy, too many people are focusing on the fat content while ignoring the total picture when thinking about their diet. Many low-fat meals are still high in calories, especially those from carbohydrates; unfortunately, when your daily intake of calories exceeds the amount your body requires, weight gain occurs, whether the calories are from fats, carbs or protein.

A widely lauded energy source, carbohydrates can lower "bad" cholesterol levels; however, a diet too high in carbohydrates coupled with a lack of sufficient exercise can not only cause weight gain but also lower the "good" cholesterol, and even promote diabetes in some people. Moderation is always the key, and most of your daily carbohydrate needs can be fulfilled with several servings each of fruits and vegetables, which are low in calories and fat.

BROWN BAGGER'S DELIGHT

Powering through the noon hour with a homemade lunch is a great way to stay on top of your paperwork—as well as your diet. But finding healthful, easy-to-prepare brown-bag fare can be difficult. The folks at Butterball have introduced a new line of luncheon meats that are all fat-free. The selections include smoked and oven-roasted turkey, bologna and hot dogs. They are lower in calories than regular cold cuts but still rank high in taste—which means they'll be a hit inside Power Ranger lunch boxes, too.

LAMB BURGERS IN PITA WITH YOGURT SAUCE

Called tzatziki *in Greece, this yogurt sauce can also be used on a baked potato as a nonfat alternative to sour cream. To prevent the pita bread in this recipe from getting soggy, place the trimmed portion of the bread down into the pocket to act as a sponge for the lamb drippings and yogurt.*

4 SERVINGS

2 cups plain nonfat yogurt
½ medium onion, chopped
½ cucumber, peeled, seeded, diced
1 tablespoon minced garlic
2 teaspoons fresh lemon juice
   Salt and pepper

1 pound ground lamb
⅔ cup fresh white breadcrumbs
½ medium onion, chopped
2 tablespoons chopped fresh parsley
4 teaspoons minced garlic
1¼ teaspoons dried oregano
4 pita bread rounds, top ¼ trimmed
   from each (tops reserved)
4 lettuce leaves

Mix first 5 ingredients together in medium bowl. Season yogurt sauce to taste with salt and pepper.

Mix lamb and next 5 ingredients in large bowl until well blended. Season generously with salt and pepper. Shape mixture into four ¾-inch-thick patties.

Preheat broiler. Place lamb patties on broiler rack and broil until cooked through, about 4 minutes per side.

Open pita bread rounds; line bottoms with trimmed tops, if desired. Place lettuce, burger, then large spoonful of yogurt sauce in each round. Serve, passing extra sauce separately.

Accompaniments

Good cooks know that even the simplest side dishes can make an everyday meal a memorable occasion. The recipes in this chapter do just that, with rare economy of calories and fat. But these recipes never stint on good taste. For example, look at the Steak House Creamed Spinach, Garlic Mashed Potatoes or Buttermilk Cornbread–all healthful but lavishly indulgent. Even the leaner-sounding sides like the Grilled Asparagus Spears, Rosemary Potatoes, or Currant-Lemon Pilaf hold forth the promise of a dish full of intriguing aromas, tastes, textures and colors.

Vegetables

Asian Eggplant

This slightly spicy side dish is excellent with grilled meat or chicken.

4 SERVINGS

½ bunch fresh cilantro, stems trimmed
5 tablespoons canned low-salt chicken broth
2 green onions, chopped
2 large garlic cloves
1 small jalapeño chili, chopped
1 tablespoon minced peeled fresh ginger

4 tablespoons peanut oil
1 1¼-pound eggplant, cut lengthwise into ¾-inch-wide slices and slices cut crosswise into ¾-inch-wide strips
1 tablespoon soy sauce
Salt and pepper

Combine cilantro, 1 tablespoon broth, green onions, garlic, chili and ginger in processor and puree until paste forms.

Heat 2 tablespoons oil in heavy large nonstick skillet over high heat until very hot. Add half of eggplant. Cover skillet and cook until eggplant is tender and beginning to brown, turning once, about 5 minutes. Transfer to paper towels. Repeat with remaining 2 tablespoons oil and remaining eggplant.

Add cilantro paste and soy sauce to skillet and stir over medium-high heat 2 minutes. Return eggplant to skillet and add remaining 4 tablespoons broth. Stir until sauce thickens and boils and eggplant is heated through, about 3 minutes. Season with salt and pepper.

Cilantro Carrots with Cumin

8 SERVINGS

2 pounds carrots, each cut into 2-inch-long pieces, then quartered lengthwise
6 tablespoons water
Salt
3 tablespoons fresh lemon juice
3 tablespoons olive oil
2 tablespoons ground cumin
2 garlic cloves, pressed
Pepper
2 tablespoons minced fresh cilantro

Combine carrots and 6 tablespoons water in large saucepan. Season with salt. Cover and boil until carrots are crisp-tender, about 7 minutes. Drain off any excess water. Transfer carrots to large shallow bowl. Mix in lemon juice, oil, cumin and garlic. Season with salt and pepper. Cool. Add cilantro. *(Can be made 2 hours ahead. Let stand at cool room temperature.)*

STEAK HOUSE CREAMED SPINACH

8 SERVINGS

1 large onion, chopped
¾ pound turkey Italian sausages, casings removed
3 10-ounce packages frozen chopped spinach, thawed, squeezed dry
1 tablespoon all-purpose flour
2 cups canned low-salt chicken broth
½ cup half-and-half
½ teaspoon ground nutmeg
   Salt and pepper

Combine onion and sausages in heavy large Dutch oven over medium heat. Sauté until sausages brown and onion is very tender, breaking up sausages with back of spoon, about 15 minutes. Add spinach; stir until all spinach liquid evaporates, about 4 minutes. Mix in flour; stir 1 minute. Add broth, half-and-half and nutmeg. Simmer until mixture is thick, stirring frequently, about 10 minutes. Season with salt and pepper.

SPRINGTIME RATATOUILLE

6 SERVINGS

1½ pounds plum tomatoes

8 tablespoons olive oil
3 medium zucchini, cut into ½-inch pieces
3 large yellow crookneck squash, cut into ½-inch pieces
2 large red bell peppers, seeded, cut into ½-inch pieces
2 medium onions, cut into ½-inch pieces
3 tablespoons finely chopped garlic
2 tablespoons chopped fresh thyme or 2 teaspoons dried
1 tablespoon chopped fresh rosemary or 1 teaspoon dried

2 small eggplants (about 2 pounds total), cut into ½-inch pieces
⅓ cup chopped fresh basil
   Salt and pepper

Blanch tomatoes in pot of boiling water 20 seconds. Drain. Peel tomatoes. Cut in half; squeeze out seeds. Chop tomatoes. Heat 5 tablespoons oil in heavy large Dutch oven over high heat. Add zucchini, crookneck squash, bell peppers, onions, garlic, thyme and rosemary. Sauté until vegetables are almost tender, about 10 minutes. Transfer to large bowl.

Heat 3 tablespoons oil in same pot over high heat. Add eggplant; sauté until just beginning to soften and brown, about 5 minutes. Add tomatoes; sauté 10 minutes. Return zucchini mixture to pot. Reduce heat; simmer until all vegetables are tender, about 15 minutes. Mix in basil. Season with salt and pepper. (*Can be made 2 days ahead. Cool, then cover and chill. Bring to room temperature before serving.*) Serve warm or at room temperature.

Jerusalem Artichokes with Rosemary

Jerusalem artichokes have nothing to do with Jerusalem or artichokes. They are, in fact, native American tubers that are part of the sunflower family. Halved and baked until golden brown, Jerusalem artichokes look like crusty roasted potatoes, but have a different, distinctive taste. Be sure the ones you choose are all about the same size so that they will be done at the same time.

8 SERVINGS

¼ cup olive oil
4 teaspoons minced fresh rosemary
    or 1½ teaspoons dried
    Salt and pepper
3 pounds Jerusalem artichokes

1 tablespoon chopped fresh parsley

Preheat oven to 425°F. Combine oil and rosemary in large bowl; season with salt and pepper. Scrub Jerusalem artichokes under cold running water (do not peel). Cut in half. Immediately add to oil mixture and toss to coat.

Arrange artichokes, cut sides down, on heavy large baking sheet. Bake until artichokes are just tender and cut sides are golden brown, about 35 minutes. Transfer to platter. Season with salt; sprinkle with parsley and serve.

Spring Stir-Fry

6 SERVINGS

12 baby red or golden beets, trimmed

4 tablespoons (½ stick) unsalted butter
1 cup packed sliced shallots
6 ounces oyster mushrooms, stems trimmed
½ pound sugar snap peas, stringed
2½ teaspoons mustard seeds
1½ teaspoons dried thyme
¾ teaspoon sugar
1½ cups thinly sliced fennel
½ cup fresh shelled peas or ½ cup frozen
4 green onions, sliced on diagonal
    into ½-inch-thick pieces
½ cup fresh Italian parsley leaves
2 tablespoons balsamic vinegar
    Salt and pepper

Cook beets in medium pot of boiling salted water until tender, about 15 minutes. Drain; cool. Peel beets and cut in half.

Melt 2 tablespoons butter in heavy large nonstick skillet over high heat. Add shallots and mushrooms; sauté 3 minutes. Add sugar snap peas; sauté 2 minutes. Mix in mustard seeds, thyme and sugar. Add 2 tablespoons butter, fennel and peas. Stir-fry 4 minutes. Add green onions, parsley, vinegar and beets; toss to blend. Season with salt and pepper.

Glazed Pearl Onions with Raisins and Almonds

This relish-like vegetable dish would go well with roast duck, goose, ham and certainly a traditional Thanksgiving turkey.

8 SERVINGS

2 pounds pearl onions

1 cup dry sherry
½ cup raisins
¼ cup honey
¼ cup water
2 tablespoons (¼ stick) butter
1 teaspoon minced fresh thyme or
  ½ teaspoon dried
  Salt and pepper
⅔ cup slivered almonds, toasted
  (about 3½ ounces)
4 teaspoons sherry wine vinegar
  or red wine vinegar

Bring pot of salted water to boil. Add onions; cook 3 minutes to loosen skins. Drain and cool slightly. Cut root ends from onions. Squeeze onions at stem end (onions will slip out of skins).

Combine pearl onions, sherry, raisins, honey, water, butter and thyme in heavy large skillet. Bring to boil over medium-high heat. Reduce heat to very low; cover and simmer until liquid evaporates and onions begin to caramelize, stirring often, about 45 minutes. Season with salt and pepper. Remove from heat. (*Can be prepared 6 hours ahead. Let stand at room temperature. Rewarm over low heat before continuing.*) Stir almonds and sherry wine vinegar into onions. Add a few teaspoonfuls of water if mixture is too dry. Serve warm.

PREVENTING VITAMIN LOSS

Fruits and vegetables are terrific sources for all of that cancer-fighting, health-building dietary good stuff. That is, they're terrific sources if all those vitamins and antioxidants don't escape before the food hits the plate. The *University of California at Berkeley Wellness Letter* reports that produce retains more nutrients when micro-waved than when boiled, steamed or baked. A Cornell University study, which confirmed the findings, suggests further ways to hold onto those valuable A's and C's: Always defrost frozen produce in the microwave instead of at room temperature, cover food to reduce microwaving time and never overcook.

BUTTERNUT SQUASH WITH ONIONS AND PECANS

8 SERVINGS

3 tablespoons butter
1 large onion, finely chopped
2¼ pounds butternut squash, peeled,
    seeded, cut into ½-inch cubes
    (about 6 cups)
    Salt and pepper
1 cup coarsely chopped pecans
    (about 4 ounces), toasted
3 tablespoons minced fresh parsley

Melt butter in heavy large skillet over low heat. Add onion and sauté until very tender, about 15 minutes. Add squash and toss to coat. Cover and cook until squash is tender but still holds its shape, stirring frequently, about 15 minutes. Season to taste with salt and pepper. *(Can be prepared 4 hours ahead. Let stand at room temperature. Rewarm over medium heat before continuing.)* Stir in half of pecans and half of parsley. Transfer to bowl. Sprinkle with remaining pecans and parsley and serve.

SEASONAL READING

Gather together a professor of medicine from Yale University and three of the hottest chefs in this country, and you get appealing recipes for today's health-conscious epicure. *Heart Healthy Cooking for All Seasons* (Pocket Books, 1996, $25) was written by Marvin Moser, M.D., who knew that quick-fix diet plans can be as disastrous as rigid, super-low-fat plans. His "fat-budgeting" strategy dishes out real food that generally stays within the national guidelines for fat and cholesterol intake.

And talk about real food—this book showcases cuisine from Alice Waters of Chez Panisse, Larry Forgione of An American Place and Jimmy Schmidt of The Rattlesnake Club. Their recipes—like summer berry and maple pancakes, and chicken grilled with lemons, garlic and artichokes—are arranged seasonally to help cooks use the freshest ingredients.

GRILLED ASPARAGUS SPEARS

The grill—and a dash of roasted garlic oil—give the asparagus terrific flavor without adding much fat. Flavored olive oils are becoming more readily available, and garlic oil can be found at most specialty foods stores and some supermarkets.

6 SERVINGS

4 cups water
2 teaspoons olive oil
1½ teaspoons roasted garlic oil or
    olive oil
1½ pounds large asparagus, trimmed
    Salt and pepper

2 tablespoons chopped fresh Italian
    parsley

Prepare barbecue (medium-high heat). Combine water, olive oil and roasted garlic oil in large bowl. Add asparagus to water mixture and toss to coat. Let stand 5 minutes. Drain. Season with salt and pepper.

Grill asparagus until crisp-tender, turning frequently, about 6 minutes. Transfer to platter. Sprinkle with parsley.

Potatoes

ROSEMARY POTATOES

Simple and low in fat.

4 SERVINGS

4 small russet potatoes

2 tablespoons olive oil
¼ cup chopped fresh rosemary
Salt and pepper

Place potatoes in medium saucepan. Cover with water; bring to boil. Boil potatoes until just tender when pierced with small sharp knife. Cool. Peel potatoes. Cut lengthwise into ½-inch-thick slices.

Prepare barbecue (medium-high heat) or preheat broiler. Brush potatoes with oil. Sprinkle with rosemary, salt and pepper. Grill potatoes until beginning to brown, about 4 minutes per side.

MASHED SWEET POTATOES AND PEARS

Pears and pear nectar add a delightful accent.

8 SERVINGS

5 pounds red-skinned sweet potatoes (yams)

6 tablespoons unsalted butter, room temperature
4 large firm but ripe Bartlett pears, peeled, cored, cut into ⅓-inch-thick slices
¾ cup (or more) pear nectar

¼ cup sugar
½ teaspoon ground cinnamon
¼ teaspoon (generous) ground cardamom
Salt and pepper

Preheat oven to 400°F. Butter 13x9x2-inch glass baking dish. Pierce potatoes in several places with fork. Place on baking sheet; bake until very tender when pierced with knife, about 1 hour. Remove from oven. Reduce temperature to 350°F.

Meanwhile, melt 2 tablespoons butter in heavy large nonstick skillet over medium-high heat. Add pears; sauté until beginning to soften, about 5 minutes. Add ¾ cup nectar; bring to simmer. Reduce heat to medium-low; cover and simmer until pears are very tender, adding more nectar if mixture sticks to skillet and stirring often, about 4 minutes. Transfer to processor and puree.

Peel sweet potatoes; place in large bowl of electric mixer. Add 4 tablespoons butter; beat until smooth. Mix in pear puree, sugar, cinnamon and cardamom. Season with salt and pepper. Transfer to prepared dish. (*Can be prepared 1 day ahead. Cover and chill.*)

Bake potatoes uncovered until just heated through, about 20 minutes.

CREOLE-STYLE OVEN HASH BROWNS

4 SERVINGS

6 large red-skinned potatoes (about 2½ pounds), peeled, cut into ½-inch pieces
1 teaspoon paprika
1 teaspoon chili powder
1 teaspoon Creole or Cajun seasoning or 1 additional teaspoon chili powder
Salt
¼ cup olive oil

Preheat oven to 400°F. Cook potatoes in medium pot of boiling salted water until almost tender, about 5 minutes. Drain well. Spread potatoes on heavy large baking sheet. Sprinkle with paprika, chili powder and Creole seasoning. Season with salt. Drizzle olive oil over potatoes and stir to coat.

Bake potatoes until crisp, turning with metal spatula every 10 minutes, about 40 minutes.

GARLIC MASHED POTATOES

There are only two tablespoons of butter in these delicious potatoes.

8 SERVINGS

3¾ pounds red-skinned potatoes, peeled, cut into 1-inch cubes
9 large garlic cloves

2 tablespoons (¼ stick) butter
2 tablespoons chopped fresh rosemary or 2 teaspoons dried
1 cup (or more) canned low-salt chicken broth
½ cup grated Parmesan cheese
Salt and pepper

Fresh rosemary sprigs (optional)

Cook potatoes and garlic in large pot of boiling salted water until both are very tender, about 30 minutes. Drain.

Transfer potatoes and garlic to large bowl. Using electric mixer, beat potatoes and garlic. Add butter and chopped rosemary; beat until smooth. Bring 1 cup broth to simmer. Gradually mix broth into potato mixture. Stir in Parmesan. Season with salt and pepper. (*Can be prepared up to 2 hours ahead. Cover. Rewarm in heavy large saucepan over medium-low heat, stirring often and adding more broth if mixture is too dry.*)

Transfer potatoes to bowl. Garnish with rosemary sprigs, if desired.

SKIP THE FAT

The folks at Oscar Mayer have made it a little easier to prepare quick and wholesome lunches for home, school and the office. Three slices of their new deli-thin ham have a mere 35 to 40 calories and no fat. Either the honey, baked or smoked variety can help make a better-for-you lunch without the fat—or guilt—of regular cold cuts.

Beans & Grains

WHITE BEANS WITH TOMATOES AND CHILIES

Serve the beans as a side dish or mix them with pasta for a light meatless meal.

4 SERVINGS

1 tablespoon olive oil
2 tablespoons chopped drained canned pickled jalapeño chilies
1½ tablespoons chopped fresh sage or 2 teaspoons dried rubbed sage
1 tablespoon chopped garlic
2 15-ounce cans cannellini (white kidney beans), drained
1¾ cups canned crushed tomatoes with added puree
Salt and pepper

Heat olive oil in heavy medium saucepan over medium heat. Add jalapeño chilies, sage and chopped garlic and sauté until garlic is tender but not brown, about 5 minutes. Add cannellini beans and tomatoes and simmer until mixture thickens and flavors blend, about 15 minutes. Season to taste with salt and pepper and serve.

BETTER BEANS

Since they're as versatile as they are healthful, beans are a perfect nutrient-packed accompaniment to just about any meal. Eden Foods has introduced a line of flavored canned beans and lentils that make it a snap to put together good-for-you, satisfying meals. For instance, their baked beans are a mix of navy beans seasoned with mustard and other spices, while the lentils have a touch of sweet onion and bay leaf. The beans are great for enhancing soups or building nutritionally complete salads. Each variety is organic and fat-free, with less sodium than many other brands. The Eden brand can be found in natural foods stores and some supermarkets.

BROWN IS BEAUTIFUL

As far as grains go, brown rice is hard to beat. Because its bran and germ are not removed, brown rice contains more fiber, iron and vitamin E than any other type of (unenriched) rice and less than one gram of fat per serving.

Right now, the USA Rice Council is distributing a free pamphlet called *Brown Rice: The Whole Grain.* Nutritious recipes like spicy southwestern chowder and mixed-vegetable pilaf highlight the rich flavor and chewy texture of this rice. For a copy, send a business-size S.A.S.E. to the USA Rice Council, Department MN, P.O. Box 740121, Houston, TX 77274.

BULGUR WITH LEEKS, CRANBERRIES AND ALMONDS

6 SERVINGS

6 tablespoons (¾ stick) butter
3 cups chopped leeks (white and pale green parts only)
5 cups canned low-salt chicken broth
3 cups bulgur*

⅔ cup dried cranberries
⅔ cup sliced almonds, toasted
Salt and pepper

Melt butter in heavy large saucepan over medium-high heat. Add chopped leeks and sauté until very tender, about 12 minutes. Add chicken broth and bring to boil. Stir in bulgur and boil 5 minutes. Add dried cranberries. Remove from heat, cover and let stand 15 minutes. Fluff with fork. Mix in sliced almonds. Season to taste with salt and pepper.

Also called cracked wheat, bulgur is available at natural foods stores and some supermarkets nationwide.

MINTED COUSCOUS WITH CURRANTS AND PINE NUTS

8 SERVINGS

2 14½-ounce cans low-salt chicken broth
6 tablespoons (¾ stick) butter
3 cups couscous
½ cup dried currants
½ cup pine nuts, toasted
4 green onions, thinly sliced
¼ cup minced fresh mint
2 tablespoons minced fresh dill
Salt and pepper

Bring broth and butter to boil in medium saucepan. Remove from heat; stir in couscous. Cover; let stand 5 minutes. Fluff couscous with fork. Transfer to bowl. Add currants, pine nuts, green onions, mint and dill; stir to blend. Season with salt and pepper.

GET REAL

A recent edition of *Consumer Reports on Health* stresses that dietary supplements are no substitute for healthful eating. Daily doses of high-priced pills meant to take the place of nutritious foods have not been shown to perform as well as a low-fat diet with plenty of fruits, vegetables and grains.

This information was further bolstered by studies reporting that beta-carotene supplements failed to reduce the risk of heart disease or cancer. Essentially, it is impossible to condense large amounts of fresh produce into a tiny capsule without losing large amounts of the nutrients that the fruits and vegetables are valued for. The best advice is to eat real food—it really works.

CURRANT-LEMON PILAF

4 SERVINGS

2 tablespoons (¼ stick) butter
½ cup minced onion
1 cup long-grain white rice
1 14½-ounce can low-salt chicken broth
½ cup water
¼ cup fresh lemon juice
2 teaspoons grated lemon peel
⅓ cup dried currants
Salt and pepper
¼ cup slivered almonds, toasted

Melt butter in heavy large saucepan over medium heat. Add onion and sauté until translucent, about 5 minutes. Add rice; stir to coat with butter mixture, about 1 minute. Mix in broth, water, lemon juice, lemon peel and currants. Bring mixture to boil, stirring occasionally. Cover pan, reduce heat to medium-low and cook until liquids are absorbed and rice is tender, about 20 minutes. Season with salt and pepper. Mix in almonds and serve.

TRAVELING COMPANION

As the demand for fresh, wholesome food grows, more and more establishments serving good-for-you meals are springing up around the country. To help you find healthful dining in an unfamiliar city (or your own neighborhood), there's *Vegetarian Journal's Guide to Natural Foods Restaurants in the U.S. and Canada* (Avery Publishing Group, 1995, $11.95). The guide lists more than two thousand cafes, juice bars and restaurants from coast to coast that cater to lovers of organic foods, healthful international cuisine and meatless dishes. Each entry indicates special menu choices, hours of operation, price range, address and phone number. Save room in your suitcase for this helpful publication.

Breads

BROWN SODA BREAD

Delicious brown bread—in loaves, cakes and scones—is the staff of life in Ireland, so addictive that travelers lug suitcases of the nutty-textured Irish brown flour as far as the tropics to ensure supplies. You can, however, make good brown bread from the harder and finer American whole wheat flour.

8 SERVINGS

1¾ cups all-purpose flour
1¾ cups whole wheat flour
 3 tablespoons toasted wheat bran
 3 tablespoons toasted wheat germ
 2 tablespoons old-fashioned oats
 2 tablespoons (packed) dark
    brown sugar
 1 teaspoon baking soda
 ½ teaspoon salt
 2 tablespoons (¼ stick) chilled
    unsalted butter, cut into pieces
 2 cups (about) buttermilk

Preheat oven to 425°F. Butter 9x5x3-inch loaf pan. Combine first 8 ingredients in large bowl; mix well. Add butter; rub in with fingertips until mixture resembles fine meal. Stir in enough buttermilk to form soft dough. Transfer dough to prepared loaf pan. Bake until bread is dark brown and tester inserted into center comes out clean, about 40 minutes. Turn bread out onto rack. Turn right side up and cool on rack.

BUTTERMILK CORN BREAD

You can make this tender corn bread a day ahead.

12 SERVINGS

 2 cups yellow cornmeal
 1 cup sifted all-purpose flour
 6 tablespoons sugar
 1 tablespoon baking powder
 ¾ teaspoon salt
 ½ teaspoon baking soda
 ½ cup (1 stick) chilled unsalted
    butter, diced
1½ cups buttermilk
 3 large eggs

Preheat oven to 400°F. Butter bottom of 9x9x2-inch baking pan. Mix first 6 ingredients in processor. Add butter and cut in, using on/off turns, until mixture resembles coarse meal. Beat buttermilk and eggs in large bowl to blend. Add cornmeal mixture to egg mixture and blend. Transfer to prepared pan.

Bake until corn bread is light golden brown on top and tester inserted into center comes out clean, about 30 minutes. Cool in pan on rack. (*Can be prepared 1 day ahead. Cover and let stand at room temperature.*)

WHOLE WHEAT SODA BREAD WITH DRIED PEARS AND ANISE

Pears add sweetness to this quick and easy anise-scented bread. It's good for toast at breakfast time.

MAKES 2 ROUND LOAVES

4 teaspoons aniseed
¼ cup anisette liqueur

4 cups whole wheat flour
2 cups unbleached all-purpose flour
1 cup old-fashioned oats
1 tablespoon salt
2 teaspoons baking soda
2¼ cups buttermilk
2 large eggs
¼ cup unsulfured (light) molasses
¼ cup (½ stick) unsalted butter, melted
1 pound dried pears, cut into ½-inch pieces

Preheat oven to 350°F. Butter heavy large baking sheet. Place 4 teaspoons aniseed in small sealable plastic bag; close bag. Using mallet, pound seeds until coarsely crushed. Combine crushed aniseed and anisette liqueur in small bowl.

Stir both flours, oats, salt and baking soda in large bowl to blend. Whisk buttermilk, eggs, molasses and melted butter in medium bowl. Whisk in anisette mixture. Make well in center of dry ingredients. Pour buttermilk mixture into well; stir until blended. Mix in pears (dough will be dense and moist).

Turn dough out onto floured surface. Knead gently until dough comes together and pear pieces are well distributed, about 2 minutes. Cut dough in half. Form each half into 6-inch round. Transfer to prepared baking sheet. Flatten slightly. Using sharp knife, cut ½-inch-deep cross in center of each round.

Bake until bread is golden and sounds hollow when tapped and tester inserted into center of bread comes out clean, about 55 minutes. Transfer to racks. Cool completely. (*Can be made ahead; wrap in foil and store at room temperature 1 day or freeze up to 2 weeks. Thaw bread; rewarm wrapped in foil in 350°F oven about 15 minutes, if desired.*)

ROBO-COOK

Thanks to the efficiency of bread machines, it takes minimal time and effort to transform humble ingredients into spectacular bakery delights. And with her *Best Low-Fat, No-Sugar Bread Machine Cookbook Ever* (HarperCollins Publishers, 1995, $16.95), Madge Rosenberg makes sure that those creations are nutritious as well as flavorful. Every loaf—including a spiced sweet potato bread, Russian pumpernickel and focaccia—is made without added fats, refined sugars or artificial sweeteners. There is also a chapter on no-salt breads and an instructive introduction about using a bread machine to its full potential.

SOUTHWESTERN CORN BREAD STUFFING

Chilies and corn—staples of the southwestern diet—are the hallmarks of this stuffing. Its intense corn flavor comes from a mixture of corn bread, corn chips, corn kernels and cream-style corn. It gets its zip from poblano and jalapeño chilies. Partner this with the Southwestern Turkey with Garlic-Ancho Chili Paste and Gravy (see Index) to bring the taste of Santa Fe to your holiday menu.

12 SERVINGS (ABOUT 15 CUPS)

Buttermilk Corn Bread (see recipe)

6 tablespoons (¾ stick) butter
1½ cups chopped onions
1½ cups chopped green bell peppers
4 large poblano chilies, stemmed, seeded, chopped
3 large jalapeño chilies, stemmed, seeded, chopped
¼ cup chopped fresh sage or 4 teaspoons dried rubbed sage
1½ tablespoons dried oregano
¾ cup chopped fresh cilantro
1½ cups crushed corn chips (such as Fritos)
1½ cups frozen corn kernels, thawed
Salt and pepper
3 large eggs, beaten to blend

1¼ cups (about) canned cream-style corn

Preheat oven to 325°F. Cut corn bread into 4 equal pieces. Crumble 3 pieces onto large baking sheet (reserve remaining piece for another use). Bake until slightly dry, about 20 minutes. Transfer to very large bowl.

Melt butter in heavy large skillet over medium-high heat. Add onions, bell peppers, all chilies, sage and oregano and sauté until vegetables are tender, about 10 minutes. Transfer to bowl with corn bread. Mix in cilantro, corn chips and corn kernels. Season to taste with salt and pepper. (*Can be prepared 1 day ahead. Cover and refrigerate.*) Mix eggs into stuffing.

TO BAKE STUFFING IN TURKEY: Fill main turkey cavity with stuffing. Mix enough cream-style corn into remaining stuffing to moisten (about ½ to ¾ cup cream-style corn, depending on amount of remaining stuffing). Spoon remaining stuffing into buttered baking dish. Cover with buttered foil. Bake stuffing in dish alongside turkey until heated through, about 40 minutes. Uncover and bake until top begins to brown, about 15 minutes.

TO BAKE ALL STUFFING IN PAN: Preheat oven to 325°F. Butter 13x9x2-inch baking dish. Mix 1¼ cups cream-style corn into stuffing. Transfer to prepared dish. Cover with buttered foil and bake until heated through, about 45 minutes. Uncover and bake until beginning to brown, about 20 minutes.

BOXTY

Made with a mixture of cooked and raw potatoes, boxty was created as a way to use a few readily available ingredients to produce different results. It can take shape as bread, pancakes or dumplings. The recipe has been popular for so long that one traditional rhyming song goes, "Boxty on the griddle, boxty on the pan; if you can't make boxty, you'll never get a man." The households that didn't have a store-bought grater improvised by using nails to punch grating holes into a box or a flattened tin can.

MAKES ABOUT 18

1 9-ounce russet potato, peeled, cut into 1-inch pieces
1¼ cups grated peeled russet potato (about one 9-ounce potato), squeezed dry in kitchen towel
¾ cup all-purpose flour
1 teaspoon baking soda
½ teaspoon salt
½ cup (about) buttermilk

Vegetable oil

Preheat oven to 300°F. Cook cut potato in saucepan of boiling salted water until tender, about 15 minutes. Drain. Return to saucepan and mash. Transfer 1 cup mashed potato to large bowl; reserve any remaining mashed potato for another use. Mix grated potato, flour, baking soda and salt into 1 cup mashed potato. Gradually mix in enough buttermilk to form texture of firm mashed potatoes.

Heat heavy large skillet over medium-high heat until hot. Brush with oil. Drop 1 heaping tablespoonful potato mixture into skillet. Using back of spoon, flatten mixture into 2-inch round. Repeat, forming 4 more rounds. Cook over medium-low heat until boxty is golden brown on bottom and slightly puffed, about 3 minutes. Turn and cook until second side is brown, about 3 minutes. Transfer to baking sheet; keep warm in oven. Repeat with remaining potato mixture in batches, brushing skillet with more oil as necessary.

IRISH OATS

The fertile soil of Ireland bears more than just potatoes. It also produces the high-quality oats used in McCann's Irish Oatmeal. This imported low-fat cereal comes in steel-cut, quick-cooking and instant varieties, so you can prepare a sensible and delicious breakfast no matter how little time you have. And oatmeal does more than just stick to your ribs; it reduces cholesterol levels and boosts iron for oxygen-rich blood.

McCann's Oat Bran earns its health-food badge as well. It has a mere one gram of fat, four grams of natural oat fiber and only 80 calories a serving. Oat bran makes a hearty breakfast cereal and can be used in muffin and bread recipes. It can also be used as a low-fat coating for meat and fish or as a thickener for soups and stews.

McCann's products are found in grocery stores nationwide.

CRUSTY BREADSTICKS WITH ROSEMARY

These Italian-style breadsticks are a deliciously different addition to a special dinner. You will need a plastic spray bottle filled with water to mist the oven while the breadsticks are baking (the water makes them crusty and chewy on the outside and slightly softer inside).

MAKES 12 BREADSTICKS

1¾ cups warm water (105°F to 115°F)
1 envelope dry yeast
　Pinch of sugar
1 tablespoon salt
1 tablespoon (generous) chopped fresh rosemary or 1 teaspoon dried
4 cups (or more) bread flour
2 tablespoons cold milk
2 tablespoons extra-virgin olive oil

　Cornmeal

12 fresh rosemary sprigs

1 egg, beaten to blend (glaze)
　Coarse salt (optional)

Place water in large bowl of electric mixer fitted with dough hook. Add yeast and pinch of sugar; stir to blend. Let stand until foamy, about 10 minutes. Add 1 tablespoon salt and chopped rosemary; beat at medium speed until blended. Add 4 cups flour, 1 cup at a time, beating until well incorporated. Mix milk and oil in small bowl. With mixer running on low speed, gradually add milk mixture. Increase speed to medium; beat 6 minutes. Scrape dough from hook and sides of bowl (dough will be soft and sticky). Let dough rest in bowl 15 minutes.

Sprinkle 2 heavy large baking sheets generously with cornmeal. Turn out dough onto floured surface and knead until soft and slightly sticky, adding more flour if necessary. Divide dough into 12 equal pieces. Let dough rest 10 minutes.

Roll each dough piece between work surface and palms of hands to 12-inch-long rope. Arrange 6 ropes on each baking sheet, spacing apart. Break small green clusters off rosemary sprigs. Insert stem end of rosemary clusters along top of breadsticks, spacing rosemary 2 inches apart. Using sprayer filled with cold water, lightly mist breadsticks. Let rise uncovered in warm draft-free area until puffy and light, about 30 minutes.

Position 1 rack in lowest third of oven and 1 rack in center and preheat to 450°F. Brush breadsticks lightly with glaze. Sprinkle very lightly with coarse salt, if desired. Place baking sheets on racks in oven and spray oven with water. Bake 15 minutes, spraying oven with water every 5 minutes. Continue baking without spraying until breadsticks are golden and sound hollow when tapped, about 15 minutes longer. Transfer breadsticks to racks; cool. (*Can be made ahead. Wrap tightly in foil and freeze up to 2 weeks. Thaw breadsticks. If desired, rewarm wrapped sticks in 350°F oven 15 minutes.*)

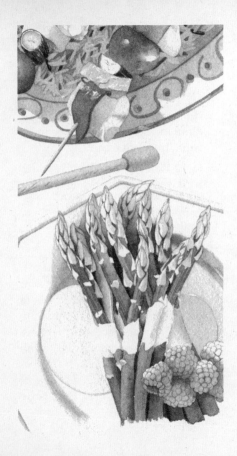

Condiments

MANGO AND RED ONION SALSA

A flavorful accompaniment for roast pork, chicken, burgers or grilled shrimp.

MAKES ABOUT 1¾ CUPS

2 small mangoes, peeled, pitted, diced
¾ cup chopped red onion
¼ cup chopped fresh cilantro
2 tablespoons fresh lime juice
1 teaspoon minced peeled fresh ginger
½ teaspoon grated lime peel
⅛ teaspoon cayenne pepper
Salt and pepper

Combine all ingredients in medium bowl; toss to blend. Season with salt and pepper. Let stand 20 minutes. (*Can be prepared 3 hours ahead. Cover and refrigerate.*)

CRANBERRY AND HORSERADISH RELISH

Here's a tangy condiment that's great with roast turkey, beef or leg of lamb.

MAKES ABOUT 3 CUPS

1 12-ounce bag fresh or unthawed frozen cranberries
1 small onion, quartered
½ cup sugar
¼ teaspoon salt
½ cup light sour cream or plain low-fat yogurt
3 tablespoons drained prepared horseradish
Salt and pepper

Combine cranberries, onion, sugar and salt in processor. Chop coarsely, using on/off turns. Transfer mixture to medium bowl. Mix in sour cream and horseradish. Season to taste with salt and pepper. Refrigerate until chilled, about 1 hour. (*Can be prepared 1 day ahead. Cover and keep refrigerated.*)

PICTURE OF HEALTH

It is a sure sign that healthful eating is here to stay when a book comes out that elevates the topic to coffee-table status. Created by the same team producing the lavish Beautiful Cookbook series, the oversize pages of the *Healthy Gourmet Cookbook* (Collins Publishers San Francisco, 1994, $45) feature more than two hundred international recipes by Pamela Sheldon Johns. The recipes are organized by season to showcase a wide variety of fresh ingredients. Each recipe is accompanied by full-color photography and includes a nutritional analysis listing calories, protein, carbohydrates, total and saturated fat, cholesterol, sodium and potassium. The introduction by registered dietitian Mary Abbott Hess provides a very informative overview of the principles of healthful cooking and eating, making the *Healthy Gourmet Cookbook* as useful as it is attractive.

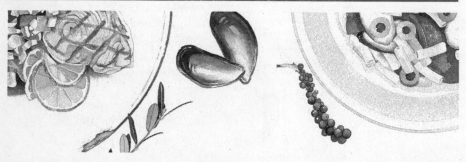

CRANBERRY-TOMATO SALSA

This creative condiment is a perfect match for Southwestern Turkey (see Index).

MAKES ABOUT 1½ CUPS

2 cups cranberries (about 8 ounces)
2 plum tomatoes, seeded, chopped
¼ cup minced cilantro
2 green onions, minced
2 tablespoons fresh lime juice
1 tablespoon (or more) sugar
2 teaspoons minced seeded jalapeño chili
1 garlic clove, minced
Salt and pepper

Cook berries in pot of boiling water until skins just begin to burst, about 1½ minutes. Drain well. Transfer to bowl. Add tomatoes, cilantro, onions, lime juice, 1 tablespoon sugar, chili and garlic. Season with salt, pepper and more sugar, if desired. (*Can be made 6 hours ahead. Cover; chill. Serve at room temperature.*)

Desserts

No one can resist "a little something sweet" to end a meal. What surprises about the recipes on the following pages is how varied they are. From fruit finales like the Blackberry Parfaits or Twelve-Fruit Compote, to frozen creations such as Chocolate Mint Sorbet or South-of-the-Border Sundaes, to baked goods like Lemon Buttermilk Cake or Cinnamon-Raisin Biscotti, the desserts in this chapter are sure to please. You're the only one who needs to know how simple and sensible they really are.

MAPLE PECAN BAKED APPLES

Try these for both dessert and breakfast. They're great with their pan juices.

6 SERVINGS

6 large Golden Delicious apples (about 3½ pounds)

⅔ cup plus 6 tablespoons coarsely chopped pecans

⅓ cup golden raisins

¼ cup sweetened flaked coconut

2 tablespoons pure maple syrup

1 teaspoon grated lemon peel

¼ teaspoon ground cinnamon

¼ teaspoon ground nutmeg

6 tablespoons peach or apricot preserves

1 cup unfiltered apple juice or cider

2 tablespoons (¼ stick) unsalted butter

Preheat oven to 375°F. Core apples.

Peel top third of each apple. Using small sharp knife, cut ¼-inch-deep line all around each where peel and flesh meet. Using small sharp knife, cut about 1¼-inch-wide, 1-inch-deep hollow in top of each apple. Cut off thin slice from bottom of each to allow apples to stand flat. Place apples in 13x9x2-inch glass baking dish.

Finely chop ⅔ cup pecans, raisins and coconut in processor. Transfer to small bowl. Mix in maple syrup, lemon peel, cinnamon and nutmeg. Divide filling equally among hollows in apples.

Spread 1 tablespoon preserves over top of each apple and into hollows. Press 1 tablespoon chopped pecans atop each.

Combine apple juice and butter in small saucepan. Stir over medium heat until butter melts. Pour into dish around apples. Cover dish loosely with foil. Bake apples 30 minutes. Remove foil; bake until apples are tender, basting with juices every 10 minutes, about 35 minutes longer. Serve apples warm with pan juices.

JUST THE FACTS, PLEASE

If you've got questions about your diet or about nutrition issues in general, the American Dietetic Association has the answers. Call their Consumer Nutrition Hot Line for a free consultation with a registered dietitian on any subject dealing with food and health, or even for a referral to a registered dietitian in your area. There are also recorded messages, updated monthly.

The recorded hot line is open weekdays from 8:00 a.m. to 8:00 p.m. (CST), and you can speak with a dietitian from 9:00 a.m. to 4:00 p.m. (CST). Call 800-366-1655.

Strawberry-Orange Compote

Terrific on its own or over angel food cake.

4 SERVINGS

1 1-pint basket strawberries, hulled, sliced
2 oranges, peel and white pith removed
1 tablespoon honey
¼ teaspoon ground cardamom

Place sliced strawberries in medium bowl. Using small sharp knife, hold oranges over same bowl and cut between membranes to release segments, allowing juice and segments to fall into bowl. Squeeze orange membranes over same bowl to release any juice. Mix in 1 tablespoon honey and ground cardamom. (*Compote can be prepared 2 hours ahead. Cover and refrigerate.*)

Summer Berries with Muscat Sabayon
(Cover Recipe)

Substituting two whole eggs for the usual four egg yolks in the custard sauce lightens this simple combination.

4 SERVINGS

1 1-pint basket strawberries, stemmed, quartered
1½ ½-pint baskets blueberries
1 ½-pint basket raspberries
4 teaspoons plus 2 tablespoons honey

½ cup orange Muscat dessert wine (such as Essensia)
2 large eggs
½ teaspoon grated orange peel
¼ teaspoon ground nutmeg

Divide berries among 4 large balloon wineglasses. Drizzle 1 teaspoon honey over berries in each glass.

Mix 2 tablespoons honey, wine, eggs, orange peel and nutmeg in medium metal bowl. Place bowl over saucepan of simmering water (do not allow bottom of bowl to touch water). Using portable electric mixer, beat until mixture holds some shape and thermometer registers 160°F, about 10 minutes.

Spoon warm sabayon over berries.

CALORIES STILL COUNT

Because of all the news about low-fat diets in the past few years, consumers might mistakenly think that any food with the words *reduced-fat* or *fat-free* on the box is going to be ideal for weight loss. However, the *Tufts University Diet & Nutrition Letter* cautions against the notion that the less-fat label is a green light for guiltless snacking.

It's true that many manufacturers have trimmed the fat in popular items, including harmful saturated fat that can lead to heart disease and possibly cancer. However, to compensate for the flavor lost with the fat, other ingredients are generally added to make the food more appealing. In so doing, the lost calories are often put back in and, in many cases, even increased beyond the original amounts. Some simple advice: Check both the fat *and* calorie totals in foods.

BLACKBERRY PARFAITS

An almond-scented pudding layered with blackberries and blackberry preserves makes a nice finale.

4 SERVINGS

¼ cup all-fruit blackberry spread
2 tablespoons amaretto liqueur
1½ teaspoons vanilla extract

⅓ cup sugar
2 tablespoons all-purpose flour
2 tablespoons cornstarch
  Pinch of salt
2¼ cups low-fat (1%) milk
1 large egg
1 teaspoon unsalted butter
¼ teaspoon almond extract

2 cups (about) frozen blackberries, thawed

Whisk blackberry spread, 1 tablespoon amaretto and 1 teaspoon vanilla in small bowl until smooth.

Whisk sugar, flour, cornstarch and salt in heavy medium saucepan to blend. Gradually whisk in milk. Whisk in egg. Add butter. Whisk over medium heat until mixture comes to boil and thickens, about 6 minutes. Boil 1 minute longer, whisking constantly. Remove from heat. Whisk in almond extract, 1 tablespoon amaretto and ½ teaspoon vanilla.

Spoon 1 teaspoon blackberry spread mixture into bottom of each of four 1-cup stemmed glasses. Top each with 4 blackberries, then with about 3 tablespoons hot pudding. Repeat layering twice more. Divide any remaining blackberries among glasses. Refrigerate until cold, about 3 hours. (*Blackberry parfaits can be prepared 1 day ahead. Keep refrigerated.*)

Pink Grapefruit with Cassis

This light, lovely dessert is a refreshing way to end a meal.

4 SERVINGS

2 large pink grapefruits (about
    14 ounces each)

2 tablespoons sugar
1½ tablespoons water
2 tablespoons crème de cassis
    Fresh mint sprigs (optional)

Using small sharp knife, remove peel and white pith from grapefruits. Working over bowl to catch juice, cut between membranes to release segments. Reserve juice in bowl. Arrange grapefruit segments decoratively on 4 plates, dividing equally.

Combine sugar, water and reserved grapefruit juice in heavy small saucepan. Stir over low heat until sugar dissolves. Remove saucepan from heat.

Stir in crème de cassis. Drizzle syrup over grapefruit. Refrigerate at least 2 hours or up to 6 hours. Garnish with mint, if desired, and serve.

Melon and Blueberry Coupe with White Wine, Vanilla and Mint

6 SERVINGS

1½ cups dry white wine
 ½ cup sugar
 1 vanilla bean, split lengthwise

2⅓ cups cantaloupe cubes
    (about ½ melon)
2⅓ cups honeydew cubes
    (about ½ small melon)
2⅓ cups watermelon cubes
    (about ¼ small melon)
 3 cups fresh blueberries
    (about 1½ half-pint baskets)
 ½ cup chopped fresh mint

Combine ½ cup wine and sugar in small saucepan. Scrape in seeds from vanilla bean; add bean. Stir over low heat until sugar dissolves and syrup is hot, about 2 minutes. Remove from heat and let steep 30 minutes. Remove vanilla bean from syrup.

Combine all fruit in large bowl. Add mint and remaining 1 cup wine to sugar syrup. Pour over fruit. Cover and refrigerate at least 2 hours. *(Can be prepared 6 hours ahead. Keep refrigerated.)* Spoon fruit and some syrup into large stemmed goblets.

Twelve-Fruit Compote

12 SERVINGS

3 cups water
1 cup sugar
1 pound mixed dried fruits
　(such as prunes, pears, apricots,
　peaches, apples and figs), cut into
　½-inch pieces
1 cup sweet white wine (such as
　Johannisberg Riesling)
1 orange, unpeeled, thinly sliced
1 lemon, unpeeled, thinly sliced
½ cup raisins
½ cup dried cherries, cranberries
　or currants
8 whole cloves
4 cinnamon sticks
1 cup seedless grapes

Combine 3 cups water and sugar in heavy large saucepan. Stir over medium heat until sugar dissolves. Add mixed dried fruits, white wine, orange, lemon, raisins, dried cherries, cloves and cinnamon sticks. Simmer compote until fruits are tender and liquid is reduced to syrup, stirring occasionally, about 20 minutes. Mix in grapes. Cool compote to room temperature; cover tightly and refrigerate. *(Can be prepared up to 3 days ahead. Keep refrigerated.)* Spoon compote into stemmed goblets and serve.

Dried Apricot Soufflés

MAKES 6 INDIVIDUAL
SOUFFLÉS

9 ounces dried apricots (about
　1½ cups)
2 cups boiling water

2 teaspoons unsalted butter, melted
3 teaspoons plus 2½ tablespoons
　sugar
5 teaspoons amaretto liqueur
2 teaspoons fresh lemon juice

5 large egg whites
　Pinch of salt
　Pinch of cream of tartar

Place apricots in large bowl. Pour boiling water over. Cover; soak apricots 2 hours.

Preheat oven to 400°F. Brush six 1¼-cup soufflé dishes with butter. Sprinkle bottom and sides of each dish with ½ teaspoon sugar. Drain apricots, reserving 3 tablespoons soaking liquid. Transfer apricots and reserved soaking liquid to processor. Puree until smooth. Blend in 1½ tablespoons sugar, amaretto and lemon juice. Transfer puree to large bowl. *(Can be made 2 days ahead. Cover and refrigerate.)*

Using electric mixer, beat egg whites, salt and cream of tartar to soft peaks in another large bowl. Gradually add 1 tablespoon sugar and beat until stiff but not dry. Stir ¼ of egg whites into apricot mixture to lighten. Gently fold remaining egg whites into apricot mixture in 2 additions.

Divide batter among prepared dishes. Place dishes on baking sheet and bake soufflés until puffed and golden on top, about 20 minutes. Serve immediately.

Cakes & Cheesecakes

ANGEL FOOD CAKE WITH STRAWBERRIES

10 TO 12 SERVINGS

1½ cups sugar
1 cup cake flour
2 cups large egg whites (about 15), room temperature
2 teaspoons cream of tartar
¾ teaspoon salt
2 teaspoons vanilla extract

Fresh sliced strawberries

Preheat oven to 350°F. Sift ½ cup sugar and flour into medium bowl 3 times. Using electric mixer, beat egg whites, cream of tartar and salt in large bowl until soft peaks form. Gradually add remaining 1 cup sugar; beat until very stiff peaks form. Fold in flour mixture in 3 additions; fold in vanilla extract. Transfer batter to ungreased 10-inch-diameter by 4-inch-deep angel food cake pan.

Bake until cake is brown and crusty on top and tester inserted near center comes out clean, about 50 minutes. Turn pan upside down and fit center onto slender bottle neck. Cool cake completely. Cut around pan sides to loosen cake. Turn cake out onto platter. Cut into wedges. Serve with strawberries.

LOW-FAT BAKING

Do double-chocolate cookies and sweet potato muffins sound as if they're out of your diet sphere? They don't have to be. The folks at Pillsbury have redefined cookies, cakes, breads and muffins in a more healthful way with their latest release, *Healthy Baking* (Viking, 1994, $23.95). The book has innovative techniques for improving over two hundred traditional and contemporary treats. By slashing the butter, shortening or oils as much as one-third, making substitutions like skim milk for whole milk, and simply eliminating the egg yolks, the authors have cut the fat, calories and cholesterol without sacrificing taste. Full-color photos accompany many of the recipes, as do nutritional charts and dietary exchange information. There are even high-altitude directions to ensure that nothing in your oven falls short of your high standards.

Chocolate-Orange Pound Cake with Coffee Glaze

A good chocolate pound cake is as versatile as a basic black dress. You can accessorize it with the glaze or simply dust it with powdered sugar. You can serve it for dessert at a dinner party or pack it for a picnic. You can give it as a gift or freeze it (for up to two months) for those times when unexpected company drops by. This one keeps at room temperature for a few days, even with the fat reduced. The glaze is a nice touch, but it's not required for your enjoyment of this cake.

12 SERVINGS

CAKE

Nonstick vegetable oil spray
1 cup plus 2 tablespoons sifted all-purpose flour
6 tablespoons unsweetened Dutch-process cocoa powder
½ teaspoon baking soda
¼ teaspoon baking powder
¼ teaspoon salt
1 large egg
2 large egg whites
2 tablespoons warm water
1 tablespoon instant espresso powder or instant coffee powder
1 teaspoon vanilla extract
6 tablespoons nonfat plain yogurt

6 tablespoons (¾ stick) unsalted butter, room temperature
1 teaspoon grated orange peel
1⅓ cups sugar

GLAZE

½ cup powdered sugar
2 tablespoons coffee liqueur

FOR CAKE: Preheat oven to 350°F. Spray 6- to 8-cup tube or Bundt pan with vegetable oil spray. Sift flour, cocoa, baking soda, baking powder and salt into medium bowl. Whisk egg and egg whites to blend in small bowl. Stir water, espresso powder and vanilla in another small bowl until powder dissolves; mix in yogurt.

Using electric mixer, beat butter and peel in large bowl for 1 minute. Gradually add sugar, beating until blended, about 3 minutes. Gradually pour eggs into butter mixture, beating until smooth, about 3 minutes. At low speed, add flour mixture alternately with yogurt mixture in 3 additions each, beating just until combined after each addition and scraping down sides of bowl. Transfer to prepared pan.

Bake cake until tester inserted near center comes out clean, about 40 minutes. Cool cake in pan on rack 10 minutes. Turn out cake onto rack; cool completely. (*Can be made 3 days ahead. Cover tightly and let stand at room temperature.*)

FOR GLAZE: Stir sugar and liqueur in small bowl until smooth. Let stand until glaze begins to set up, about 30 minutes. Spoon glaze over cake.

CAROB VERSUS CHOCOLATE

If you sometimes reach for a carob candy bar thinking it's better for you than one made of chocolate, you might want to reconsider. The carob sweet does have an initial advantage, since its base, carob flour, gets only 2 percent of its calories from fat (as opposed to about 50 percent for unsweetened cocoa powder or milk chocolate).

But according to the *University of California at Berkeley Wellness Letter,* the advantage is minimized when fat is added to carob to simulate the taste and texture of chocolate. Typically, the fat used is hydrogenated palm kernel oil (an 85-percent-saturated oil). The result? Candy that is generally not much (if at all) lower in fat than chocolate.

LEMON BUTTERMILK CAKE WITH STRAWBERRIES

Serve this dense, moist cake with a big bowl of lightly sweetened strawberries.

12 SERVINGS

CAKE

1³⁄₄ cups sugar
³⁄₄ cup (1½ sticks) unsalted butter, room temperature
2 tablespoons grated lemon peel
3 extra-large eggs
¼ cup fresh lemon juice
3 cups cake flour
1 teaspoon baking soda
¼ teaspoon salt
1½ cups buttermilk

1 16-ounce package frozen sliced sweetened strawberries, thawed

FROSTING

12 ounces cream cheese, room temperature
½ cup (1 stick) unsalted butter, room temperature
2 cups powdered sugar
5 tablespoons frozen lemonade concentrate, thawed
½ teaspoon finely grated lemon peel

2 1-pint baskets strawberries, hulled

FOR CAKE: Position rack in center of oven and preheat to 350°F. Butter and flour three 9-inch-diameter cake pans with 1½-inch-high sides. Beat sugar, butter and lemon peel in large bowl until light and fluffy. Add eggs 1 at a time, beating well after each addition. Beat in lemon juice. Sift flour, baking soda and salt into medium bowl. Stir dry ingredients into butter mixture alternately with buttermilk, beginning and ending with dry ingredients.

Divide batter among prepared pans. Bake until tester inserted into center of cakes comes out clean, about 30 minutes. Transfer pans to racks and cool 15 minutes. Turn out cakes onto racks and cool completely. (*Can be prepared 1 day ahead. Wrap tightly in plas-*

tic and store at room temperature.)

Boil sliced sweetened strawberries with juices in heavy small saucepan over medium-high heat until mixture is reduced to ⅔ cup and begins to thicken, stirring frequently, about 20 minutes. Cool to room temperature.

FOR FROSTING: Beat cream cheese and butter in large bowl until light and fluffy. Gradually add powdered sugar and beat until smooth. Beat in lemonade concentrate and lemon peel.

Divide strawberry mixture between 2 cake layers and spread over tops, leaving ½-inch border around edges. Let stand until slightly set, about 5 minutes. Place 1 strawberry-topped layer on platter. Drop ¾ cup frosting atop cake by spoonfuls; gently spread over top. Top with remaining strawberry-topped layer. Drop ¾ cup frosting atop cake by by spoonfuls atop cake; gently spread over top. Top with remaining cake layer. Using spatula, spread remaining frosting in decorative swirls over sides and top of cake.

(Can be prepared 1 day ahead. Cover with cake dome and chill. Let cake stand at room temperature 1 hour before continuing.)

Decoratively arrange strawberries, pointed side up, atop cake. Cut into wedges and serve.

MARGARITA CHEESECAKE
Made with reduced-fat cream cheese and light sour cream, this cheesecake is irresistible—just like its namesake cocktail.

10 TO 12 SERVINGS

CRUST
Nonstick vegetable oil spray
1¼ cups graham cracker crumbs
¼ cup (½ stick) unsalted butter, melted

FILLING
3 8-ounce "bricks" Neufchâtel cheese (reduced-fat cream cheese), room temperature
1¼ cups light sour cream

¾ cup plus 2 tablespoons sugar
2½ tablespoons triple sec or other orange liqueur
2½ tablespoons tequila
2½ tablespoons fresh lime juice
4 large eggs

TOPPING
¾ cup light sour cream
1 tablespoon fresh lime juice
1 tablespoon sugar

Very thin lime slices, cut in half
Very thin lime peel strips

FOR CRUST: Position rack in center of oven and preheat to 350°F. Spray 9-inch springform pan with 2¾-inch-high sides with vegetable oil spray. Mix graham cracker crumbs and butter in medium bowl until blended. Press crumbs over bottom and 1 inch up sides of prepared pan. Refrigerate crust.

FOR FILLING: Using electric mixer, beat cheese in large bowl until fluffy. Beat in sour cream, then sugar, triple sec, tequila and lime juice. Beat in eggs.

Pour filling into crust. Bake until outside 2 inches are set and center moves only slightly when pan is shaken, about 50 minutes. Remove from oven; turn off oven.

FOR TOPPING: Whisk sour cream, lime juice and sugar in small bowl to blend. Spread evenly over cheesecake. Return cheesecake to hot oven. Let stand 45 minutes. (Cheesecake will look very soft but will set up when chilled.) Refrigerate cake until well chilled, up to 1 day.

Run knife around pan sides. Remove pan sides. Place cake on platter. Arrange lime half-slices and peel around top edge of cheesecake.

TROPICAL COCONUT CHEESECAKE

Rum replaces butter in the crust, and light cream cheese is used in the filling and light sour cream in the topping. All work to reduce the fat in this cheesecake without reducing the rich flavor and texture associated with a favorite treat.

12 SERVINGS

CRUST

9 whole graham crackers (each with 4 sections)
3 tablespoons golden brown sugar
2½ tablespoons (or more) dark rum

FILLING

1½ pounds chilled light cream cheese
1 cup packed golden brown sugar
3 large eggs
1 teaspoon imitation coconut extract

TOPPING

1 cup light sour cream
2 tablespoons sugar
1½ tablespoons dark rum

3 mangoes, peeled, pitted, sliced
Apricot jam (glaze)

FOR CRUST: Preheat oven to 350°F. Finely grind graham crackers with sugar in processor. Add 2½ tablespoons rum and process until crumbs are just moist, adding more rum by ½ teaspoonfuls if mixture is dry. Using paper towel as aid, press crumb mixture onto bottom of 9-inch-diameter springform pan with 2¾-inch-high-sides. Bake crust until dry and slightly puffed, about 12 minutes. Cool on rack. Maintain oven temperature.

FOR FILLING: Using electric mixer, beat cream cheese and sugar in large bowl until smooth. Add eggs 1 at a time, beating just until blended after each addition. Mix in extract. Pour filling into crust. Bake cake until filling begins to puff and crack around edges and center moves only slightly when shaken, about 40 minutes. Remove cake from oven; maintain oven temperature.

FOR TOPPING: Mix sour cream,

sugar and rum in small bowl. Spread topping evenly over hot cheesecake. Bake 5 minutes. Transfer cake to rack and cool completely. Cover cake with foil and refrigerate overnight.

Run knife around pan sides to loosen cake. Release pan sides. Overlap mango slices decoratively atop cake. Stir jam in small saucepan over low heat until melted. Brush jam over fruit.

CHOCOLATE-MOCHA CHEESECAKE

It's hard to believe that this luscious marbled cheesecake is low in fat and calories, but it's true. The absence of a crust, the use of light cream cheese and low-fat cottage cheese, and the substitution of unsweetened cocoa powder for pure chocolate make all the difference.

12 SERVINGS

Nonstick vegetable oil spray

1 **16-ounce container low-fat (2%) small-curd cottage cheese**

1 **8-ounce "brick" Neufchâtel cheese (reduced-fat cream cheese), room temperature**

1¼ **cups sugar**

1 **tablespoon vanilla extract**

2 **teaspoons instant espresso powder or instant coffee powder**

¼ **teaspoon salt**

3 **large eggs, room temperature**

6 **tablespoons unsweetened Dutch-process cocoa powder**

Position rack in lowest third of oven and preheat to 350°F. Line bottom of 8-inch-diameter cake pan with 2-inch-high sides with parchment paper. Spray sides of pan with vegetable oil spray.

Blend cottage cheese in processor until silky smooth, scraping down sides occasionally, about 3 minutes. Add Neufchâtel cheese and blend well. Add 1 cup sugar, 1 tablespoon vanilla extract, 2 teaspoons espresso powder and salt and blend well. Add 3 eggs and process just until smooth. Pour 2 cups of coffee batter into spouted measuring

cup. Add 6 tablespoons cocoa powder and remaining ¼ cup sugar to batter in processor and blend well.

Pour 1¾ cups cocoa batter into prepared pan. Pour coffee batter directly into center of cocoa batter (coffee batter will fill center, pushing cocoa batter to edge). Pour remaining cocoa batter directly into center of coffee batter. Run small knife through batters to create marbled pattern. Set cake pan into 13x9x2-inch baking pan. Pour enough boiling water into baking pan to come halfway up sides of cake pan. Set baking pan in oven.

Bake cake until edges just begin to puff and crack and center is just set, about 50 minutes. Remove cake from baking pan and set on rack to cool. Refrigerate cake until cold, about 6 hours; cover tightly. *(Can be prepared 2 days ahead; keep refrigerated.)*

Cut around pan sides to loosen cake. Cover pan tightly with plastic wrap, then cover with cardboard round or tart pan bottom. Invert cake onto plastic and cardboard. Hold pan and cardboard together tightly and rap firmly to release cake. Lift off cake pan. Peel off parchment. Place serving platter on cake. Invert cake onto platter. Lift off cardboard; peel off plastic wrap. Refrigerate until ready to serve.

Pastries & Cookies

RAISIN AND CARDAMOM GRANOLA BARS

MAKES 18

2 cups old-fashioned oats
½ cup packed brown raisins
½ cup chopped pecans, toasted
1¼ teaspoons ground cardamom
6 tablespoons (¾ stick) unsalted butter
⅓ cup packed dark brown sugar
3 tablespoons honey

Preheat oven to 350°F. Line 9-inch square baking pan with foil, allowing foil to extend over sides. Butter foil. Mix oats, raisins, pecans and cardamom in bowl. Combine butter, sugar and honey in medium saucepan. Stir over medium heat until butter melts and mixture is smooth and begins to boil. Pour butter mixture over oat mixture and stir until well coated. Transfer to prepared pan. Using spatula, press mixture evenly into pan.

Bake oat mixture until top is golden brown, about 30 minutes. Transfer to rack and cool. Using foil as aid, lift out of pan; place on work surface. Using large sharp knife, cut into 18 bars.

PHYLLO TARTLETS WITH LIME CURD AND BOYSENBERRIES

A standard curd filling is loaded with calories and is high in fat. But the one in this dessert calls for an egg substitute like Egg Beaters instead of the egg yolks, and cornstarch to replace the butter.

4 SERVINGS

CURD

⅓ cup sugar
1 teaspoon cornstarch
⅓ cup Johannisberg Riesling or other semisweet white wine
⅓ cup fresh lime juice
1 teaspoon grated lime peel
½ cup egg substitute (real egg product)

TARTLETS

4 sheets fresh phyllo dough or frozen, thawed
2 tablespoons (¼ stick) unsalted butter, melted
4 teaspoons (generous) sugar

1 cup frozen boysenberries or
blackberries, thawed, drained
3 tablespoons sugar
2 cups fresh boysenberries

FOR CURD: Mix sugar and cornstarch in heavy medium saucepan until no lumps remain. Mix in wine, lime juice and lime peel. Whisk in egg substitute (mixture may appear curdled). Whisk mixture over medium heat until thick and just beginning to boil, about 7 minutes. Immediately transfer curd to small bowl; cool. Cover and refrigerate overnight.

FOR TARTLETS: Lightly butter four ³⁄₄-cup custard cups or ramekins. Stack phyllo sheets on work surface. Trim to 12-inch square. Cut 12-inch square into four 6-inch-square stacks. Lightly butter 1 phyllo square (cover remaining phyllo with plastic and damp towel). Sprinkle with generous ¼ teaspoon sugar. Lightly butter second phyllo square; sprinkle with sugar. Place second phyllo square atop first square, turning second square slightly so that corners point in different directions. Repeat with 2 more phyllo squares, placing each at a different angle atop others. Gently press stack of phyllo squares into 1 prepared custard cup, forming pastry tulip. Repeat process with remaining phyllo squares, butter and 3 teaspoons sugar, forming 3 more pastry tulips. Chill 30 minutes.

Preheat oven to 350°F. Place custard cups on baking sheet. Bake until pastries are golden brown, about 20 minutes. Cool.

Puree 1 cup thawed berries and 3 tablespoons sugar in blender. Strain puree into bowl. Mix in 2 cups fresh berries. *(Pastries and sauce can be made 6 hours ahead. Let pastries stand at room temperature. Chill sauce.)*

Spoon curd into pastry cups, dividing equally. Top with sauce.

LIGHT INDULGENCES

When the weather is cold, rainy or just generally gloomy, baking cookies is one of the best ways to pass the time indoors. Hershey's can help you make the resulting treats lighter without losing any of the richness. Their new reduced-fat chocolate baking chips have 50 percent less fat and 25 percent fewer calories than the regular chips, but all the taste of traditional Hershey's chocolate. Try the recipes on the package for fudge, cookies and other desserts, or enjoy the chips straight from the bag with a little less guilt.

CARAMEL AND CHOCOLATE RASPBERRY NAPOLEONS

Sometimes a little magic is needed to get things just right. After substituting phyllo leaves for the traditional butter-loaded puff pastry used in napoleons and subtracting rich milk or cream from the usual custard recipe, these raspberry napoleons were very light indeed—but they were not nearly good enough for a dessert. In the end, the phyllo was caramelized for a nice crunch and a thin layer of intense bittersweet chocolate was added—perfection.

6 SERVINGS

CUSTARD

3 tablespoons sugar
4 teaspoons all-purpose flour
4 teaspoons cornstarch
1 large egg
1 large egg yolk
1 cup low-fat (1%) milk
1 teaspoon vanilla extract

PHYLLO PASTRIES

4 14x18-inch fresh phyllo pastry sheets or frozen, thawed
4 teaspoons melted unsalted butter
16 teaspoons sugar

1½ ounces bittersweet (not unsweetened) or semisweet chocolate, finely chopped

2 ½-pint baskets raspberries

FOR CUSTARD: Stir 3 tablespoons sugar, 4 teaspoons flour and 4 teaspoons cornstarch in small bowl until no lumps remain. Add egg and egg yolk and whisk until thick and smooth. Bring 1 cup low-fat milk just to simmer in heavy medium saucepan. Gradually whisk hot milk into egg mixture. Return mixture to same saucepan and whisk over medium heat until custard thickens and boils 1 minute. Strain custard into medium bowl. Whisk in 1 teaspoon vanilla extract. Place plastic wrap directly onto surface of custard and refrigerate custard until very cold, at least 3 hours and up to 2 days.

FOR PHYLLO PASTRIES: Position rack in center of oven and preheat to 375°F. Line heavy large baking sheet with parchment paper. Place 1 phyllo sheet on work surface; keep remaining sheets covered with kitchen towel. Brush phyllo sheet with 1 teaspoon melted unsalted butter, covering sheet completely. Sprinkle 1 teaspoon sugar over. Top with another phyllo sheet; brush with 1 teaspoon butter and sprinkle with 1 teaspoon sugar. Cut stack lengthwise into 3 equal strips, about 4½x18 inches each. Stack 3 strips together, making one 6-layer strip. Cut strip crosswise into six 4½x3-inch rectangles. Repeat with remaining 2 phyllo sheets (for a total of twelve 4½x3-inch rectangles of 6 layers each). Using large spatula, transfer phyllo rectangles to prepared baking sheet. Cover phyllo with large parchment sheet, then with another baking sheet to act as weight.

Bake 5 minutes. Remove top baking sheet and top sheet of parchment. Bake phyllo until dark golden brown, turning baking sheet twice for even baking and watching closely to keep from burning, about 5 minutes longer. Transfer phyllo rectangles to racks and cool. (*Can be prepared 2 days ahead. Store phyllo rectangles in airtight container at room temperature.*)

Preheat broiler. Sprinkle each phyllo rectangle with scant 1 teaspoon sugar. Place 1 phyllo rectangle on baking sheet and broil close to heat source until sugar melts and turns amber, turning frequently and watching closely, about 20 seconds. Transfer phyllo rectangle to rack and cool (sugar topping will become crisp). Repeat broiling process with remaining phyllo rectangles.

Stir bittersweet chocolate in top of double boiler over simmering water until melted and smooth. Remove from heat. Using fork tines, drizzle melted chocolate decoratively over 6 caramelized rectangles; reserve as top

layers. Spread remaining melted chocolate in even layer over caramel on remaining 6 phyllo rectangles. Refrigerate 6 chocolate-covered phyllo rectangles just until chocolate sets.

Place 6 chilled chocolate-covered phyllo rectangles on work surface. Spread about 2 tablespoons custard over chocolate on each. Arrange as many raspberries as will fit on custard. Spread 1 tablespoon custard on bottom side of each reserved phyllo top and place custard side down on raspberries, pressing gently to adhere. (*Can be prepared 1 hour ahead. Refrigerate.*)

CINNAMON-RAISIN BISCOTTI

These crisp, low-fat cookies are just right for dipping into dessert wine or cappuccino.

MAKES ABOUT 2 DOZEN

1 large egg
½ cup sugar
1 tablespoon brandy
1 teaspoon vanilla extract
¾ cup plus 2 tablespoons
  all-purpose flour
¾ teaspoon baking powder
¾ teaspoon ground cinnamon
¼ teaspoon (generous) salt
⅓ cup raisins
⅓ cup whole almonds, toasted

Preheat oven to 375°F. Lightly grease heavy large baking sheet. Using hand-held electric mixer, beat egg and sugar in medium bowl until very thick and fluffy, about 2 minutes. Beat in brandy and vanilla. Sift flour, baking powder, cinnamon and salt into egg mixture and blend well. Mix in raisins and almonds. Spoon dough onto prepared sheet to form 10- to 11-inch strip. Using moistened fingertips, shape dough into neat 11-inch-long by 2½-inch-wide log.

Bake until log just begins to brown and feels firm to touch, about 20 minutes. Cool cookie log on sheet 15 minutes. Maintain oven temperature.

Transfer cookie log to work surface. Using serrated knife, cut crosswise into ⅓-inch-wide slices. Arrange slices on same baking sheet. Bake 10 minutes. Turn slices over. Bake until beginning to color, about 8 minutes longer. Cool cookies completely on baking sheet (cookies will become very crisp). *(Can be prepared 1 week ahead. Store in airtight container at room temperature.)*

SHERLOCK HEALTH

Researchers from New York University did some detective work in Manhattan convenience stores recently. They looked at the stated weights of those baked goodies—cookies, brownies and cake slices—that are individually wrapped in cellophane and placed in checkout lines to cash in on impulse shoppers.

As reported by the *Tufts University Diet & Nutrition Letter,* the researchers found that, although national brands were generally accurate in listing the weights of their products, a number of the locally baked products showed a marked difference between actual and stated weights—sometimes more than an ounce.

What does that mean to consumers? A hundred or more extra calories. *Tufts* reports that since these types of snacks ordinarily have around a hundred calories an ounce, understating the weight significantly understates the calorie count—and the amount of fat. The newsletter advises readers to be mindful of those inviting treats near the cash register; if you're concerned about extra calories, you might want to look elsewhere for a snack.

Frozen Desserts

CHOCOLATE MINT SORBET WITH MINT COOKIES

The low-fat cookies look pretty when rolled into cylinders, but they are just as nice (and easier to make) if they are left flat. Extras are great with coffee or tea. There is plenty of chocolate taste but little fat in the sorbet.

4 SERVINGS

SORBET

2 cups water

¾ cup plus 2 tablespoons sugar

1 ounce bittersweet (not unsweetened) or semisweet chocolate, chopped

½ cup unsweetened cocoa powder

2 tablespoons light corn syrup

2 teaspoons vanilla extract

¼ teaspoon peppermint extract

COOKIES

Vegetable oil spray

2 large egg whites

¼ cup all-purpose flour

3 tablespoons sugar

1 teaspoon minced fresh mint

1 teaspoon vanilla extract

¼ teaspoon peppermint extract

1½ tablespoons butter, melted

1 ½-pint basket fresh raspberries

FOR SORBET: Combine water and sugar in heavy small saucepan. Stir over low heat until sugar dissolves. Increase heat and bring mixture to boil. Remove from heat. Add chocolate and stir until melted. Add cocoa, corn syrup and extracts and whisk until smooth. Chill 1 hour.

Transfer chocolate mixture to ice cream maker and process according to manufacturer's instructions. Freeze sorbet in covered container.

FOR COOKIES: Preheat oven to 325°F. Spray heavy nonstick baking sheet with vegetable oil spray. Whisk egg whites in medium bowl until beginning to foam. Add flour, sugar, minced mint and extracts to batter. Whisk until smooth; whisk in butter.

Drop 1 level tablespoon batter near each end of prepared baking sheet. Using back of small spoon, spread each tablespoon of batter to 4½- to 5-inch round. Bake cookies until light brown but still soft, about 7 minutes. Loosen cookies gently with edge of spatula and turn over. Bake cookies until brown, about 4 minutes longer. Using wooden spoon handle and pot holder as aids, tightly roll 1 cookie at a time around handle, forming narrow tube. Slide cookie off handle; cool. Let baking sheet cool. Repeat baking and rolling with remaining batter, forming 2 cookies per batch (10 cookies total) and cooling baking sheet between batches. (*Sorbet and cookies can be made 1 day ahead. Keep sorbet frozen. Store cookies airtight.*)

Scoop sorbet into dessert dishes. Serve each with berries and 1 cookie.

CHOCOLATE SNACKS

Along with all that cereal, the Quaker Oats Company is one of the foremost producers of those light and airy rice cakes—which are either a boon or a curse for between-meal snackers, depending on where you're coming from. Now, Quaker Oats has added *the* taste to these guiltless wonders: Chocolate Crunch. Each serving (one large cake or five mini ones) has no fat and only 50 calories. They're an ideal way to tame afternoon hunger pangs.

MINT JULEP SORBET

A treat for mint julep fans. Traditional silver mint julep cups or frozen parfait glasses add a nice accent at serving time.

4 SERVINGS

1½ cups water
¾ cup (lightly packed) fresh mint leaves (from about 2 small bunches)
½ cup sugar

3 tablespoons bourbon
1 tablespoon green crème de menthe
1 teaspoon minced fresh mint leaves

4 fresh mint sprigs

Combine first 3 ingredients in heavy large saucepan. Stir over medium heat until sugar dissolves. Increase heat and bring to boil. Pour into medium bowl. Refrigerate until cold, about 2 hours.

Strain mint syrup through sieve set over bowl, pressing on mint leaves. Discard mint leaves. Mix bourbon, crème de menthe and minced mint leaves into mint syrup. Process sorbet mixture* in ice cream maker according to manufacturer's instructions. Transfer sorbet to container; cover and freeze until firm, about 2 hours. (*Can be prepared 2 days ahead; keep frozen.*)

Freeze 4 parfait glasses for 1 hour. Scoop sorbet into frozen glasses. Garnish with mint sprigs; serve immediately.

*To make this into a granita, mix an additional ½ cup water into sorbet mixture. Freeze until semifirm, whisking occasionally, about 3 hours. Cover and freeze until solid, at least 6 hours or overnight. Using fork, scrape surface of granita to form crystals. Scoop crystals into frozen glasses; serve immediately.

LIME MARGARITA SORBET

This dessert is a refreshing way to conclude a spicy southwestern meal. For a festive note, dip the rims of frozen Margarita glasses into water and then into a bowl of sugar. Attach a lime slice to the lip of the glass and fill with sorbet.

4 SERVINGS

2 cups water
1 cup sugar
⅔ cup fresh lime juice
6 tablespoons triple sec
6 tablespoons tequila
1 teaspoon grated lime peel

Stir water and sugar in heavy medium saucepan over medium heat until sugar dissolves. Increase heat and bring to boil. Pour into medium bowl. Mix in lime juice, triple sec, tequila and lime peel. Refrigerate until cold, about 2 hours.

Transfer sorbet mixture* to ice cream maker and process according to manufacturer's instructions. Transfer sorbet to container; cover and freeze until firm, about 2 hours. (*Can be prepared 2 days ahead. Keep frozen.*)

Freeze 4 Margarita glasses for 1 hour. Scoop sorbet into frozen glasses and serve immediately.

*To make this into a granita, mix an additional 1 cup water into sorbet mixture. Freeze in bowl until semifirm, whisking occasionally, about 3 hours. Cover and freeze until solid, at least 6 hours or overnight. Using fork, scrape surface of granita to form crystals. Scoop crystals into frozen glasses and serve granita immediately.

PRALINE SUNDAES WITH PLUM VANILLA SAUCE

Using frozen yogurt for the sundaes instead of a premium ice cream reduces the fat in each serving by one-third.

6 SERVINGS

2 pounds Santa Rosa or other red-fleshed plums, pitted, chopped
1 vanilla bean, split lengthwise
¾ cup sugar
¼ cup water
½ cup hazelnuts, toasted, chopped
1 tablespoon brandy
1 pint vanilla frozen yogurt, slightly softened
3 plums, halved, pitted, sliced

Puree chopped plums in blender until smooth. Press puree through sieve into bowl. Transfer 1½ cups puree to small saucepan. (Reserve remaining puree for another use.) Scrape seeds from vanilla bean into saucepan with puree.

Lightly oil baking sheet. Stir sugar and water in another small saucepan over low heat until sugar dissolves. Increase heat to high and boil without stirring until syrup is deep brown, brushing down sides of pan with wet pastry brush and swirling pan occasionally.

Working quickly, pour half of caramel into plum puree (caramel will harden on contact). Set aside. Immediately mix hazelnuts into remaining caramel in pan. Scrape nut mixture onto oiled baking sheet. Let stand until completely cool. Coarsely chop praline.

Stir puree in saucepan over medium heat until caramel melts, about 2 minutes. Transfer plum sauce to bowl; cool. Mix in brandy. (*Praline and sauce can be prepared 2 days ahead. Store praline airtight at room temperature. Cover sauce and refrigerate.*)

Finely chop enough praline to measure ¼ cup. Wrap tightly and reserve. Fold remaining coarsely chopped praline into frozen yogurt; freeze until firm, at least 1 hour and up to six hours.

Spoon some plum sauce into bottom of each of 6 stemmed glasses. Top with half of plum slices, then 2 small scoops vanilla frozen yogurt. Spoon remaining plum sauce over. Top sundaes with remaining plums and reserved praline and serve.

SOUTH-OF-THE-BORDER SUNDAES

Store-bought vanilla frozen yogurt acts as the luscious foil for oranges, pineapple, mango and bananas in a fat-free brown sugar-cinnamon sauce.

8 SERVINGS

4 oranges
¾ pineapple, peeled, cored, cut into bite-size pieces
1 large mango, peeled, pitted, cut into bite-size pieces

½ cup plus 2 tablespoons firmly packed dark brown sugar
½ teaspoon ground cinnamon

3 bananas, peeled, sliced
1½ pints vanilla frozen yogurt

Using zester, remove peel in long strips from 1 orange; reserve peel. Cut white pith from orange. Cut peel and pith from remaining oranges. Working over bowl to collect juices and using small knife, cut between membranes of 1 orange to release segments. Transfer segments to large bowl. Squeeze juice from orange membranes into bowl with juices. Repeat with remaining oranges. Add pineapple and mango to orange segments.

Combine ⅓ cup juice collected from oranges, reserved orange peel, brown sugar and cinnamon in small saucepan. Stir over low heat until sugar dissolves. Increase heat and boil until mixture thickens slightly, about 1 minute. Discard peel. Mix syrup into fruit. (*Can be made 4 hours ahead. Cover and chill.*)

Mix bananas into fruit. Scoop frozen yogurt into bowls. Spoon fruit mixture and juices over and serve.

Ice Cream Sodas with Lime, Mint and Ginger

This cross between a fizz and a float—a new take on an old-fashioned treat—is a lovely warm-weather refreshment.

6 SERVINGS

1½ cups sugar
 1 cup fresh lime juice
 ¾ cup chopped fresh mint
 2 tablespoons chopped fresh ginger

 6 cups (about) chilled sparkling water
1½ pints (about) vanilla frozen yogurt
 Lime slices (optional)
 Fresh mint sprigs (optional)

Combine sugar, lime juice, chopped mint and ginger in heavy large saucepan. Stir over medium heat until sugar dissolves and syrup comes to simmer. Simmer syrup 2 minutes. Remove from heat and cool completely. Strain syrup into small bowl, pressing lightly on solids; discard solids. (*Can be prepared 1 week ahead. Cover and refrigerate.*)

Pour 3 tablespoons syrup, then ¾ cup sparkling water into each of 6 tall glasses. Stir to blend. Mix in additional syrup or sparkling water to taste. Top each with 1 scoop vanilla frozen yogurt. Garnish sodas with lime slices and mint sprigs, if desired, and serve.

Blackberry and Hazelnut Sundaes

Hazelnut liqueur adds zip to the sauce in this easy dessert.

4 SERVINGS

⅓ cup sugar
⅓ cup (packed) golden brown sugar
⅓ cup water
 2 tablespoons butter
 3 tablespoons Frangelico (hazelnut liqueur) or amaretto
⅓ cup hazelnuts (about 2 ounces), toasted, husked, chopped

 Vanilla frozen yogurt
1 ½-pint basket fresh blackberries

Combine sugar, brown sugar and water in heavy small saucepan. Stir over medium-low heat until both sugars dissolve. Add butter and stir until melted. Increase heat and boil until sauce is reduced to ½ cup, about 4 minutes. Remove from heat. Mix in Frangelico and nuts. (*Can be prepared 1 day ahead. Let stand at room temperature. Before using, stir over low heat until heated through and smooth.*)

Scoop frozen yogurt into bowls. Spoon warm sauce over. Top with berries.

PINEAPPLE SPLIT

The classic goes tropical in this luscious rendition featuring pineapple and coconut.

6 SERVINGS

1 cup tropical, mango, guava or papaya fruit nectar

½ cup sugar

1 fresh pineapple, peeled, halved lengthwise, cored, each half cut crosswise into 9 half-moon slices

1½ pints (about) tropical-flavored sorbet (such as mango, banana, coconut or pineapple)

1 cup shredded sweetened coconut, toasted

Fresh mint sprigs

Stir nectar and sugar in heavy medium saucepan over high heat until sugar dissolves and syrup comes to boil. Boil until syrup is reduced to ⅔ cup, about 5 minutes. Cool syrup completely (syrup will thicken as it cools). (*Can be prepared 1 day ahead. Cover and let stand at room temperature.*)

Overlap 3 pineapple slices to form ring on each of 6 plates. Place 1 scoop sorbet in center of each ring. Drizzle syrup over, then sprinkle generously with coconut. Garnish with mint.

JUST WHAT THE DOCTOR ORDERED

Developed by a team of heart specialists from Stanford University, *The Stanford Life Plan for a Healthy Heart* (Chronicle Books, 1996, $29.95) is a total nutrition program. It aims to limit saturated-fat intake to less than 25 grams a day and to keep cholesterol levels in check to help prevent heart disease.

The first half of this hefty volume offers "The Fat Tracker's Guide," which shows how to locate and avoid too much fat in the products that you purchase, cook with and eat. It also includes several week-by-week models demonstrating how to cut back on fats gradually.

The second half features more than two hundred low-fat recipes, such as salmon salad with tangerines, cucumbers and ginger-lemon dressing; chili with white beans and grilled chicken; and spicy couscous with yams, carrots and onions.

Index

Acknowledgements & Credits

Recipes supplied by:

Megan Baskin
Mary Barber
Caroline Belk
Rosalind Bergeron
Patrick Bermingham
Davina Besford
Veronica Betancourt
Lena Cederham Birnbaum
Marilyn Bright
Susan Burnside
Lucy Carney
Alice Colin
Sara Corpening
Amy Willard Cross
Lane Crowther
Liza Davies

Dorothy Davis
Gretchen Davis
Tony DiSalvo
Maguy Maccario-Doyle
Janet Fletcher
Jim Fobel
Dr. Lance Fogan
Lucy Footlik
Gerri Gilliland
Ken Haedrich
Lynn Hagee
Janet Hazen
Alan Herman
Janie Hibler
Wendy Hutzler
Jean Jamieson
Elizabeth Johnson

Barbara Karoff
Karen Kaplan
Jeanne Thiel Kelley
Kristine Kidd
Jennifer A. Kirkgaard
BA Test Kitchen
Norman Kolpas
Deanna Herman-Kulsuptrakul
Ellen Lebow
Jessica Leighton
Idelle Levey
Tony Litwinko
Alice Medrich
Carmela Meely
Selma Brown Morrow
Peggie O'Kennedy
Patti Robbins

Betty Rosbottom
Sharon Ryan
Carolyn Schmitz
Martha Rose Shulman
Joy Smith
Richard Snyder
Scott Snyder
Galit Stevens
Sarah Tenaglia
Marjorie Thompson
Michael Thompson
Wayne Turett
Karen Turner
Lorraine Vassalo
Charlotte Walker
Andrea Webster
Janet R. White

Text:

Anthony Head
Katie O'Kennedy
Laurie Glenn Buckle
Tanya Wenman Steel

Concept:

Tamra Febesh
Jennifer Capaccio

*Editorial development and
  original writing:*
Norman Kolpas

Graphic design:
Sandy Douglas

Illustrations:
Michelle Burchard

Index:
Barbara Wurf

Proofreader:
Katie Goldman

Rights and permissions:
Sybil Shimazu Neubauer

Typography:
TeleText Typography, Inc.

BON APPÉTIT®
Light, Fresh & Easy